Best Value Books™

Table of Contents

Parts of Speech

Grammar Grades 7-8

Prepared by: Kelley Wingate Levy
Written By: Dr. Vicki Gallo Sullivan

This book is just one in our Best Value™ series of reproducible, skill oriented activity books. Each book is developmentally appropriate and contains over 100 pages packed with educationally-sound, classroom-tested activities. Each book also contains skill cards and resource pages with extended activity ideas.

The activities in this book have been developed to help students master the basic skills necessary to succeed in grammar. The activities have been sequenced to help insure successful completion of the assigned tasks, thus building positive self-esteem, as well as the self-confidence students need to meet academic challenges.

The activities may be used by themselves, as supplemental activities, or as enrichment material for a grammar program.

Developed by teachers and tested by students, we never lost sight of the fact that if students don't stay motivated and involved, they will never truly grasp the skills being taught on a cognitive level.

About the author...

Dr. Vicki Gallo Sullivan has spent twenty-plus years in the business/art of educating children. With areas of specialization in reading, curriculum and instruction, and gifted education, she has run the teaching gamut from elementary and secondary to the university level. Her direct experience with children ranges from classroom teacher and Reading Specialist to Chapter 1 Coordinator and Gifted Resource Instructor. She has taught curriculum courses for over a decade at several universities in Louisiana. Dr. Sullivan has also served as an External Assessor in the Louisiana Teacher Assessment Program.

Outside the field of education, Dr. Sullivan works as a travel consultant in a family-owned and run travel agency. Being deeply stricken with wanderlust herself, she often shares her enthusiasm for both foreign and domestic destinations. Much of the subject matter in this book is a direct result of her travels.

Ready-to-Use Ideas and Activities

The activities in this book will help children master the basic skills necessary to become competent learners. Remember as you read through the activities listed below and as you go through this book, that all children learn at their own rates. Although repetition is important, it is critical that we never lose sight of the fact that it is equally important to build children's self-esteem and self-confidence if we want them to become successful learners.

Skill card ideas

The back of this book has removable skill cards that will be helpful for basic skill and enrichment activities. Pull the skill cards out and cut them apart (if you have access to a paper cutter, use that). Following are several ideas for use of the skill cards.

Have students write sentences that summarize a story or lesson. Use the **parts of speech cards (#1-8)** to sort the words used in the sentences.

Take out the **verb tense cards (#9-14)** and twenty-five **sentence skill cards (#15-39).**

1. Have students place each verb card in the correct tense category. As a group, check the verbs in each category.

2. Shuffle the verb tense cards and place face up on the table. Shuffle the sentence cards and place face up next to the verb tense cards. The student should number a piece of paper from one to 25. Each student takes one verb tense and one sentence card from the top of the deck. The task is to change the sentence so the verb will match the verb tense card. Write the new sentence on the paper. Continue until all the sentences have been rewritten.

3. Have students write all eight verb tenses **(#9-14)** using verbs you supply. (example: marry, graduate, tell, travel, finish)

4. Have students use the verb tense cards to help them find and identify all six tenses in newspaper or magazine articles.

Ready-to-Use Ideas and Activities

Select the **subject and predicate skill cards (#40-54)**.

1. Have students create sentences that demonstrate each type of subject and predicate combination on the flash cards.

2. Have students find each type of subject and predicate combination in magazine or newspaper articles. Highlight or cut out the sentences and place them under the correct card.

3. Have students write five to ten simple subject and simple predicate sentences. Use the subject and predicate flash cards to expand the sentence as the flashcard dictates. For example:
   simple sentence: Students reviewed.
   flashcard #48: Students reviewed thoroughly for the exam.
   flashcard #49: The serious students reviewed.
   flashcard #50: Students and teachers reviewed.
   flashcard #51: The serious students reviewed thoroughly for the exam.
   flashcard #52: Students reviewed thoroughly for the exam and practiced for a long time.
   flashcard #53: Students and teachers reviewed and practiced.
   flashcard #54: The serious students and their worried teachers reviewed thoroughly for the exam and practiced for a long time.

Select the **sentence pattern cards (#55-59)** and the **sentence cards (#70-79)**.

1. Match the sentences with the correct pattern.

2. Have students write their own sentences that match the five sentence patterns.

3. Shuffle the sentence pattern cards and place upside-down on the table. Repeat with the sentence cards. Students take turns selecting a pattern card and drawing sentences until they find a match.

Ready-to-Use Ideas and Activities

Select the **diagraming cards (#60-66)** and the **sentence cards (#70-79)**.

1. Have the students make two diagrams for each of the sentence cards. One will be the basic sentence pattern parts and the other will contain all modifiers (adjectives, adverbs, and prepositional phrases).

2. Have the students write two original sentences that fit in each basic diagram category. Diagram each.

3. Using the student sentences constructed in the above activity (2), have them add modifiers and construct a second sentence diagram that includes the modifiers.

Select the **clause cards (#82-83)** and the clauses **(#84-96)** .

1. Individually or in pairs, have the students separate each clause into the correct "dependent" or "independent" stack. Check the work as a group.

2. Have the students rewrite the clauses **(#84-96)**. For the independent clauses, have them expand the sentence by adding a dependent clause. Have the students add an independent clause to the dependent clauses to create a complete sentence.

3. Pair the students. They are to each write five independent clauses and exchange papers. The partners add a dependent clause to each sentence. This can also be reversed, beginning with dependent clauses.

4. Have the students find ten examples of dependent clauses in newspapers, magazines, and catalogs. Highlight the sentence and underline the dependent clause.

5. Cut dependent clauses from newspapers, magazines, and catalogs. Have students write a new independent clause for each dependent clause.

Identification of Nouns

A noun names a person, place, or thing. Nouns can name specific or general persons, places, and things. They can also name ideas as well as things which can be perceived through the senses.

Example: <u>Mary</u> is my best <u>friend</u>.
Only <u>boys</u> go to that <u>school</u>.
The <u>subject</u> of the <u>book</u> was <u>democracy</u>.

Underline each noun in the narrative that follows.

The Neutral Ground

A few years before Louisiana became a state in 1812, there was a famous boundary dispute between the United States and Spain. During that period the United States had acquired the Louisiana Territory, and Spain was in control of what is now Texas. To settle the boundary dispute a neutral strip was created in 1806 in an agreement between General James Wilkerson of the United States and the Spanish commander at Los Adaes. The land was located between the Sabine River to the west and the Calcasieu River to the east. It was known as the Neutral Ground, or "No Man's Land."

Neither the laws of the United States nor the laws of Spain applied to this forty-mile-wide region. Therefore, it was a large area of ungoverned territory that attracted all kinds of people. Outlaws of both nations quickly settled in the area. Judges sometimes even sentenced criminals to the Neutral Ground. Holdups were frequent for travelers heading west through the strip. Slaves were attracted to the area with the promise of freedom, but outlaws such as Jean Lafitte the pirate captured and sold them. Some people in the area were actually former outlaws trying to start a new life where the law could not touch them.

It had been warned from the beginning that this territory would be the home of every kind of smuggler and outlaw known to man. This warning proved to be very true. It took a total of fifteen years for the boundary dispute to be settled. The Neutral Ground was finally given to the United States in 1819, but the legacy of lawless activity did not instantly disappear just because an agreement was signed.

Common and Proper Nouns

A proper noun names a particular person, place, or thing and must always be capitalized. Nouns that are not proper nouns are common nouns.

Example: (Chip) is my <u>cousin</u> who lives in the <u>state</u> of (Idaho.)

proper   common   common   proper

In each sentence circle the proper nouns and underline the common nouns.

1. The Aegean Sea is located between Greece and Turkey.

2. The capital of the state of Texas is Austin.

3. The mountain range called the Alps is not only located in the country of Switzerland, but also in France, Germany, Austria, and Italy.

4. The largest exhibit of paintings and sketches by Vincent Van Gogh is on display in a museum in Amsterdam.

5. Beethoven, the renowned composer, was born in Bonn, Germany.

6. The subject of vampires is widely explored in books and in movies.

7. President Thomas Jefferson sent expeditions to explore the territory called the Louisiana Purchase.

8. The Trojan War is reputed to have started as the result of a beauty contest between the goddesses Minerva, Juno, and Venus.

9. Times Square is in the heart of the theatre district in New York .

10. The Arenal Volcano erupts regularly in Costa Rica.

11. A flight on the Concorde will take you from New York to Paris in four hours.

12. The abacus is the oldest calculating machine known to man.

13. The San Diego Zoo is one of the most famous in the United States.

14. Mardi Gras, the French Quarter, and great food draw many tourists to New Orleans.

Compound Nouns

A compound noun is a combination of two or more words to form a new word that is used as a single noun. Some compounds are written as one word (*earring*). Others are hyphenated (*forty-one*). Others are written as two or more words (*ice cream*).

Look at each compound word below. Leave it as is if the word does not need a hyphen or separation. Rewrite it if the word does need a hyphen or separation. Use a dictionary to make sure your answers are correct.

1. **boxseat** _____

2. **mailbox** _____

3. **timeout** _____

4. **safetypin** _____

5. **pogostick** _____

6. **printout** _____

7. **showoff** _____

8. **fatherinlaw** _____

9. **photocopy** _____

10. **motherofpearl** _____

Write sentences using compound nouns other than the ones listed above.

1. _____

    _____

2. _____

    _____

3. _____

    _____

Possessive Nouns

To make a singular noun **possessive**, add *'-s*. If the noun ends in *-s* and is plural in meaning, add only an apostrophe. If the noun is singular in meaning but ends in *-s*, add *'-s*. If a plural noun does not end in *-s* the possessive is formed by adding *-'s*.

Noun not ending in -s	Noun ending in -s	Irregular Plurals
the boy	the boys	children
the *boy's* baseball	the *boys'* baseball	*children's* toys
the boss	the bosses	
the *boss's* temper	the *bosses'* meeting	
Maxine		
Maxine's book		

The singular form of the noun is given. Write the other three forms.

Singular	Singular Possessive	Plural	Plural Possessive
book	*book's*	*books*	*books'*
1. tent			
2. shoe			
3. tree			
4. violin			
5. story			
6. raccoon			
7. picture			
8. tale			
9. cup			
10. calendar			
11. baker			
12. pencil			
13. boss			

Possessive Nouns

The singular form of the noun is given. Write the other forms requested.

Singular	Singular Possessive	Plural	Plural Possessive
book	*book's*	*books*	*books'*
1. machine	_____	_____	_____
2. horse	_____	_____	_____
3. daffodil	_____	_____	_____
4. beach	_____	_____	_____
5. chair	_____	_____	_____
6. dancer	_____	_____	_____
7. novel	_____	_____	_____
8. postcard	_____	_____	_____
9. airplane	_____	_____	_____
10. musical	_____	_____	_____
11. chef	_____	_____	_____
12. paper	_____	_____	_____
13. class	_____	_____	_____
14. couch	_____	_____	_____
15. pencil	_____	_____	_____

Nouns Functioning as Subjects

Nouns and pronouns can function as the subject of the sentence. To decide if a word is the subject, ask *who* or *what* followed by the verb. The noun is called the simple subject. The subject usually precedes the verb, but not always.

Example: <u>Mary</u> runs five miles daily.
The tall, blonde <u>runner</u> is going to the Olympics.
A <u>competition</u> is always held in the spring.

Underline the noun that is the subject in each sentence.

1. Salvador went on a whale watching tour out of Half Moon Bay in California.

2. The weather was cold and windy.

3. The passengers on the boat waved good-bye.

4. The tour guide explained the migratory habits of grey whales.

5. The selected area for viewing was about one hour from shore.

6. The cold, rough winds made the trip rather uncomfortable.

7. Many people got seasick.

8. After no sightings for two hours, the captain decided to return to shore.

9. Most people were terribly disappointed.

10. The seasick people were not disappointed when they turned back toward the shore.

11. Suddenly, three whales were spotted together.

12. The immense mammals rose powerfully out of the water over and over.

13. The tourists were mesmerized by their encounter.

14. Even the most seasick woman managed to get a good look.

15. During the return to shore the marine biologist talked very seriously about endangered species such as these.

Nouns as Simple Subjects and Noun Phrases as Complete Subjects

Nouns and pronouns can function as the subject of the sentence. To decide if a word is the subject, ask *who* or *what* followed by the verb. A noun without its modifiers is called the **simple subject**. A noun with its modifiers is called a noun phrase and becomes the **complete subject**. Noun phrases include adjectives, adverbs that intensify the adjectives, and prepositional phrases. They extend and complete the noun's meaning in various ways.

Example: Mary runs five miles daily. (simple subject)
The tall girl in the blue shorts is going to the Olympics. (complete subject)

Underline the simple subject in each sentence. Circle the complete subject.

1. The moonless, brisk night was perfect for Halloween.

2. The howling wind added to the effect.

3. Hooting owls could be heard in the treetops.

4. Wild-eyed black cats roamed through the streets.

5. Scary yard decorations were evident everywhere.

6. The excited children in their scary costumes ran from house to house.

7. A boy in a mummy costume had the largest bag for treats.

8. A vampire with glistening fangs walked beside him.

9. The cackling laughter of a tall witch made them scatter.

10. The triumphant witch watched the two boys run for the safety of a porch.

11. Two cute little skeletons knocked on Mr. Burke's door.

12. A ghost in a white sheet opened the door.

13. Homemade cookies in orange trick-or-treat bags were given to each child.

14. A prissy ballerina in a pink tutu walked by with her mother and a werewolf.

15. Laughing children ran from house to house with their bags of treats.

Nouns Functioning as Predicate Nominatives

The **predicate nominative** is a noun or pronoun that follows a linking verb and renames or gives more information about the subject. It answers the question *Who* or *What is*. The linking verb describes a condition, not an action. The most common linking verb is *to be* in its various forms (*am, is, was,* and *were*) as well as *to become*.

Example: Langston Hughes was a great <u>poet</u>.

Read the sentence. Underline the predicate nominative once. Underline the linking verb twice. Draw an arrow from the predicate nominative to the subject it renames. If there is no predicate nominative, skip the sentence.

1. Jody's pet in Rawling's novel *The Yearling* is a playful and affectionate young deer.

2. The woman at the center of controversy in *The Tales of King Arthur* was Guinevere.

3. *The Outsiders* by S.E. Hinton is a dramatic novel for young teens narrated by a character named Ponyboy.

4. Charles Dickens is the author of the classic favorite *Oliver Twist*.

5. Beth is currently reading *The Little Prince*.

6. George Orwell's *Animal Farm* is an allegory that uses farm animals to illustrate the dangers of totalitarian government.

7. The Newbery Medal is awarded to the best piece of children's literature every year.

8. *The Old Man and the Sea* by Ernest Hemingway is a deceptively simple story of an old man's battle with a giant marlin.

9. The main character in Tolkein's *The Hobbit* is a far-wandering creature named Bilbo Baggins.

10. Homer's story of the Trojan War, *The Iliad*, has been a fixture in libraries and book stores all over the world for many years.

11. *Alice's Adventures in Wonderland, Through the Looking Glass*, and *What Alice Found There* were all written by Lewis Carroll.

12. *Death Be Not Proud* is a beautifully written memoir by John Gunther about his son.

Nouns Functioning as Direct Objects

A noun (or pronoun) used as a **direct object** tells *who* or *what* receives the action of the verb. A verb can have more than one direct object.

> Example: I saw <u>Marie</u>.
> John saw the <u>movie</u> and its <u>sequel</u>.

Underline the direct object in each sentence. Circle the verb. Leave the sentence blank if there is no direct object.

1. Betty recently toured Australia.

2. A big highlight of the trip for her was the colony of fairy penguins on Phillips Island.

3. On the way from Melbourne to Phillips Island, she had parsnip soup for lunch at a delightful farm.

4. Betty fed bread to kangaroos and a peacock there.

5. She also met an unforgettable wombat at the farm.

6. Betty next visited the Koala Conservation Center on the island.

7. She could reach the lower treetops by means of ramps for better viewing of koalas.

8. Luckily, she did not see the local ten foot worm that also lived in the conservation center.

9. Betty saw her first fairy penguin at Nobby's Point.

10. This 17"-tall penguin had a beautiful bluish back and a white belly.

11. She saw many fairy penguins coming out of the sea in groups of three to twenty-five.

12. Many of them were carrying fish back to their mates on land.

13. Betty could actually see the females patting their returning mates in apparent appreciation for the meal.

14. At dinner that night she saw a picture of a 21' shark that was captured right off Nobby's Point.

Nouns Functioning as Indirect Objects

A noun (or pronoun) that tells *to whom* or *for whom* the action of the verb is done is called the **indirect object**. One verb may refer to more than one indirect object. A sentence containing an indirect object must also contain a direct object.

> Example: I gave <u>Sally</u> a dollar. (direct object—dollar; indirect object—Sally)
> I gave <u>Sally</u> and her <u>sister</u> a ride to school. (direct object—ride;
> indirect objects—Sally and sister)

Underline the indirect object(s) in each sentence. Circle the verb. Underline the direct object twice.

1. Marcy gave her teacher a bouquet of flowers.

2. Aunt Alice sends Drew a birthday present every year.

3. My teacher taught the class facts about solar energy today.

4. Ben Franklin High School offers its students a strong college prep curriculum.

5. I told my youngest sister a bedtime story.

6. Beverly showed her best friend a picture of her new love.

7. Alex told Roxanne a big secret.

8. Every summer the Smiths send their daughter a box of goodies at her camp.

9. The professor taught his students French.

10. Alice wrote her pen pal a detailed letter every month.

11. Joseph bought his fiancée a diamond engagement ring.

12. Patricia showed the producers her considerable talent at the audition.

13. Robert refused Milly her request.

14. The drunken pirate showed the young boy a treasure map.

15. The wealthy man showed the beggar some unaccustomed kindness.

Nouns Functioning as Objects of Prepositions

A noun (or pronoun) or noun phrase often follows a preposition to form a prepositional phrase. The **preposition** shows relationships between the noun and some other words in the sentence. The noun is called the object of the preposition. Some of the most common prepositions include *about, across, around, at, before, between, by, down, during, for, from, inside, into, of, on, over, under,* and *with*.

> Example: Albany is the capital of <u>New York</u>. (shows relationship of capital to *New York*)
> The cat ran under the <u>bed</u>. (shows relationship of ran to *bed*)

Circle each preposition. Underline each object of the preposition.

1. She speaks with a lovely French accent.

2. On the top shelf you will find the psychology books.

3. The mail arrives at approximately four o'clock.

4. She stood stubbornly at the door.

5. The Miller family lives in the suburbs of Los Angeles.

6. The new teacher is from the state of Utah.

7. I can't travel during the summer.

8. We will leave at midnight.

9. Wait until dark.

10. The owner's manual comes with the computer.

11. The hurricane is moving across the Atlantic seacoast.

12. Valerie lives across the street in the red brick house.

13. Michelle is from a small town in France.

14. During the intermission we stood on the balcony of the theater.

15. I left my homework on my desk at home.

16. The accident resulted in a broken leg.

Nouns Functioning as Appositives

An **appositive** is a type of noun or noun phrase that identifies the same person or object by another name. It is usually enclosed in commas and immediately follows the noun it identifies. It renames the subject or predicate nominative. If the first noun is unclear without the help of the appositive, commas are not used.

Example: Julie, <u>a great dancer</u>, got the role of the Sugar Plum Fairy.
My friend <u>Anais</u> got the role of Clara.

Read the two sentences. Underline the part in the second sentence which can be used to expand the first sentence. Rewrite the first sentence so that it has an appositive when expanded.

Example: 1. Julie got the role of the Sugar Plum Fairy.
Julie is <u>a great dancer</u>.
Julie, a great dancer, got the role of the Sugar Plum Fairy.

2. My friend got the role of Clara.
My friend is <u>Anais</u>.
My friend Anais got the role of Clara.

1. **Ms. Sharon Ramsey is our choice for senator.**
Ms. Sharon Ramsey is a reform candidate.

_____

_____

2. **The United Nations is based in New York City.**
The United Nations is the most influential international organization.

_____

_____

3. **Mark just made a remarkable discovery in the Andes Mountains.**
Mark is a paleontologist.

_____

_____

Nouns Functioning as Appositives

Read the two sentences. Underline the part in the second sentence which can be used to expand the first sentence. Rewrite the first sentence so that it has an appositive when expanded.

Example: Julie got the role of the Sugar Plum Fairy.
Julie is <u>a great dancer</u>.
Julie, a great dancer, got the role of the Sugar Plum Fairy.

1. **The car was vandalized in the parking lot.**
    The car was a luxury convertible.

    _____

    _____

2. **Carla designed the itinerary for our trip to Alaska.**
    Carla is a very experienced travel consultant.

    _____

    _____

3. **Mary Shelley's novel is a great classic tale of horror.**
    Mary Shelley's novel is *Frankenstein*.

    _____

    _____

4. **The word was misused in this sentence.**
    The word is *disinterested*.

    _____

    _____

5. **Agoraphobia often affects depressed women.**
    Agoraphobia is the fear of being in open spaces.

    _____

    _____

Noun Functions Review

Look at the underlined noun. Decide its function in the sentence. Write S for subject, DO for direct object, IO for indirect object, PN for predicate nominative, OP for object of the preposition, or A for appositive.

_____ 1. Julie Andrews' remarkable <u>voice</u> was first discovered when she was nine years old.

_____ 2. She came from a family with a theatrical <u>background</u> in the English Music Hall tradition, although no one before her achieved Julie's level of success.

_____ 3. At the age of thirteen, Julie gave the royal <u>family</u> a solo performance in London.

_____ 4. At 23, she crossed the <u>Atlantic</u> in order to pursue a career on Broadway.

_____ 5. Her first theatrical smash hit was *My <u>Fair</u> <u>Lady</u>*.

_____ 6. Her co-star in *My Fair Lady* was <u>Rex Harrison</u>.

_____ 7. Her most famous movie role was probably <u>Maria</u> in *The Sound of Music*.

_____ 8. *The Sound of Music* made Julie a household name all over the <u>world</u>.

_____ 9. *<u>The Sound of Music</u>* was based on the true story of a famous Austrian woman and the events in her life at the beginning of World War II.

_____ 10. The pinnacle of Julie's movie career thus far would probably be her <u>Oscar</u> for best actress in the movie *Mary Poppins*.

_____ 11. One of her funniest <u>performances</u> was in *Victoria, Victoria*.

_____ 12. <u>Julie</u> starred in *Victor, Victoria* both in the movie and on Broadway.

_____ 13. Julie herself was particularly fond of her <u>role</u> as Guinivere in the musical *Camelot*.

_____ 14. Her live performances always demonstrate the full <u>range</u> of her vocal and acting abilities.

_____ 15. Additionally, she is the <u>author</u> of a popular children's novel called *Mandy* written under the name of Julie Edwards.

Noun Functions Review

Look at the underlined noun. Decide its function in the sentence. Write S for subject, DO for direct object, IO for indirect object, PN for predicate nominative, OP for object of the preposition, or A for appositive.

The Eastern and Oriental Express

The Eastern and Oriental Express, called the E & O, is a luxurious Asian <u>train</u> that goes
                                                                                    1
from <u>Bangkok</u> to Singapore. The <u>train</u> is a deluxe railway <u>experience</u>, and there are few of
        2   3   4
these left in the world today.

Although it was built in Japan in 1971, its <u>style</u> is purposefully reminiscent of the
                                              5
1930's. The forest green and yellow E & O contains a <u>locomotive</u> and eighteen <u>carriages</u>.
                                                          6   7
The luxurious <u>interior</u> is designed for first-class rail <u>travel</u>. The <u>train</u> has an open obser-
                 8   9   10
vation deck, a lavish formal dining car, some sleeper suites paneled in cherry wood and

elm burl, and a pale ash-paneled lounge car complete with <u>piano</u>.
                                                               11
The train leaves Bangkok, Thailand and soon the <u>temples</u> mixed with <u>skyscrapers</u> are
                                                     12   13
left behind. A watery <u>landscape</u> with only occasional teak <u>houses</u> follows. On the second
                         14   15
day, the train is in <u>Malaysia</u>, and the <u>scenery</u> changes to tidy <u>villages</u> and water buffalo.
                       16   17   18
The passengers get off the train briefly at Penang Island. Here they get to ride in a

<u>trishaw</u>, a three-wheeled vehicle, that is propelled by a pedaling driver.
  19
The train then starts ascending as it heads into the mountainous highland region of

Malaysia. <u>Rainforests</u> filled with <u>monkeys</u> narrowly line the <u>train</u>. The <u>passengers</u> take a
             20   21   22   23
30-minute midnight stop in Kuala Lumpur, the capital of <u>Malaysia</u>. Finally, two days later,
                                                           24
the train pulls into the <u>station</u> in Singapore.

1. _____	6. _____	11. _____	16. _____	21. _____
2. _____	7. _____	12. _____	17. _____	22. _____
3. _____	8. _____	13. _____	18. _____	23. _____
4. _____	9. _____	14. _____	19. _____	24. _____
5. _____	10. _____	15. _____	20. _____	25. _____

Personal, Indefinite, and Demonstrative Pronouns

Pronouns take the place of nouns. Here are three kinds:
1. **Personal pronouns** include forms of first, second, and third person: *I, mine, me, we, ours, us, you, yours, he, she, it, his, hers, its, him, her, they, theirs,* and *them.*
    Example: <u>They</u> are the best of friends.
2. **Indefinite pronouns** refer to persons or things generally. *Anybody, few, most, neither, no one, nothing,* and *several* are some indefinite pronouns.
    Example: <u>No one</u> said a word.
3. **Demonstrative pronouns** refer to persons or things specifically: *this, that, these,* and *those.*
    Example: Don't eat <u>those.</u>

Underline the pronoun used in each sentence. Identify it as P (personal), I (indefinite), or D (demonstrative).

_____ 1. Mary doesn't know anyone in the room.

_____ 2. You can't be serious.

_____ 3. He is out of the race.

_____ 4. My father doesn't trust them.

_____ 5. It won't staple.

_____ 6. Max will play chess with you.

_____ 7. Neither was prepared for the pop quiz.

_____ 8. They filled the stadium to watch the contending ice skaters.

_____ 9. The teacher won't recognize these.

_____10. Unless Beth goes, I won't.

_____11. These belong to Patrick.

_____12. Just a few won't hurt.

_____13. I brought several.

_____14. Brandy could see nothing in the dim light.

_____15. These are Joey's favorite cookies.

Interrogative and Relative Pronouns

Interrogative pronouns are used to ask questions. **Relative pronouns** introduce dependent clauses in sentences. (A dependent clause contains a subject and verb, but does not stand alone as a complete thought.) Except for *that* which is relative, but not interrogative, these pronouns are identical in form. These pronouns include *who, whom, whoever, whomever, which, what, whatever,* and *whichever.*

Example: <u>Who</u> is your first choice? (interrogative)
The girl <u>who looks upset</u> is my sister. (relative pronoun in dependent clause)

If the underlined pronoun is interrogative, write I in the blank. If the underlined pronoun is relative write R in the blank. Underline the clause that goes with the relative pronoun.

_____ 1. I will bring <u>whatever</u> you request.

_____ 2. <u>Whatever</u> is the matter with you?

_____ 3. <u>Which</u> essay won?

_____ 4. The essay <u>which</u> was written by Alyssa won.

_____ 5. Choose <u>whichever</u> you want.

_____ 6. <u>What</u> is the title of that song?

_____ 7. I don't know <u>what</u> she said.

_____ 8. <u>Who</u> betrayed my confidence?

_____ 9. I will always remember the nurse <u>who</u> was so kind.

_____ 10. The child <u>whom</u> I saw was about five years old.

_____ 11. <u>Whom</u> did you see at the parade?

_____ 12. The person to <u>whom</u> I gave my donation is the director of the campaign.

_____ 13. For <u>whom</u> is this gift intended?

_____ 14. <u>Whoever</u> could be responsible for this problem?

_____ 15. I will invite <u>whoever</u> you like.

_____ 16. Melissa gets <u>whatever</u> she wants.

_____ 17. <u>What</u> happened here?

_____ 18. Do you know <u>what</u> time it is?

_____ 19. <u>Who</u> was on the answering machine?

_____ 20. I know to <u>whom</u> the brooch belongs.

Possessive Pronouns

The personal pronouns *mine, yours, his, hers, ours*, and *theirs* show possession. Apostrophes are not used with possessive pronouns as they are with possessive nouns.
    Example: That ice cream cone is <u>mine</u>.

The personal pronouns *my, your, her, its, our*, and *their* show possession, but are always followed by nouns.
    Example: That is <u>my</u> ice cream.

The personal pronoun *his* may or may not be followed by a noun.
    Example: That is <u>his</u> ice cream.
               That ice cream is <u>his</u>.

Write a possessive pronoun in each blank to complete the sentences. Circle any nouns that follow the possessive pronoun.

1. That wallet is _____.

2. _____ friend is a salesclerk here.

3. I thought it was _____.

4. We gave the winner _____ approval.

5. _____ apology is not accepted.

6. Is this jacket _____?

7. This is _____ jacket.

8. My locker was locked, and I did not have _____ key.

9. This is _____ room.

10. The best disciplined dog in the show is _____.

11. _____ excuse sounded pretty flimsy.

12. I'm sorry that I spilled coffee on _____ dress.

13. We all took a long rest after _____ exhaustive ordeal.

14. _____ explanation sounded reasonable.

Nominative and Objective Case in Pronouns

The case of a pronoun depends on its use in the sentence. The **nominative case** includes the subject, predicate nominative, and appositive. The pronouns used in the nominative case include *I, you, he, she, it, we,* and *they*. The **objective case** includes the direct object, indirect object, and object of the preposition. The pronouns used in the objective case include *me, you, him, her, it, us,* and *them*.

Example: I know <u>them</u>. (subject and direct object)
Jeff gave <u>me</u> that letter. (indirect object)
<u>It</u> was <u>I</u> who told the teacher. (subject and predicate nominative)
The present was for <u>him</u>. (object of the preposition)

Circle the correct pronoun in the nominative or objective case. Write its function in the blank. Choose S for subject, PN for predicate nominative, A for appositive, DO for direct object, IO for indirect object, or OP for object of the preposition.

_____ 1. One winter evening (we, us) went ice skating together.

_____ 2. You and (she, her) need to finish your homework.

_____ 3. Next year's student council president might be (he, him).

_____ 4. Our best volleyball players are (they, them).

_____ 5. Call (I, me).

_____ 6. Call (she, her).

_____ 7. We showed (they, them) the treasure map.

_____ 8. The teacher watched (he, him) hand out papers.

_____ 9. The bat hit (I, me) right in the nose.

_____10. The usher escorted (they, them) to the seats.

_____11. She sat next to Amy and (I, me).

_____12. We walked toward (they, them).

_____13. The traffic guard stopped and glared at Jake and (I, me).

_____14. I gave (he, him) a slice of my homemade pecan pie.

_____15. Give the directions to (she, her).

Action Verbs

The verb states something about the subject. A verb that expresses action is called an **action verb**.

Example: The snake <u>slithered</u> under the log.
             The snake <u>slithered</u> under the log, and then it <u>reappeared</u>.
             That snake has <u>startled</u> me for the last time! (an auxiliary verb can
             accompany the action verb)

Underline the action verb in each sentence. Circle the subject.

1. Valerie loves creative gardening.

2. The search for new additions to her garden goes on and on.

3. For instance, yesterday she spotted a wild aster in the brush of a vacant lot.

4. She gently pulled up the aster by its roots.

5. Valerie tucked the flower beside a fuzzy goldenrod in her side yard.

6. The whole yard is brimming with black-eyed susans, sunflowers, and honeysuckle.

7. A pond in the center is filled with water lilies and frogs.

8. Her passion for wildflowers is also demonstrated throughout her garden.

9. She has transformed her yard into a haven for the native flora and associated wildlife.

10. Her choices of plants lure birds, butterflies, and bugs with their nectar and berries.

11. They offer shelter with safe branches and scrubby brambles.

12. Every plant grows as if it has a special purpose.

13. She reads everything available on gardening.

14. Migratory birds and mockingbirds often fly through her little haven.

15. Residential birds like cardinals and bluejays spend their lives there.

16. A bed of bright flowers attracts butterflies and bees.

17. Wild animals are not the only animals tempted by the garden.

18. Youngsters come to Valerie's home for seeds and advice.

19. People from all over town come with thoughtful additions for her garden.

20. They proudly watch their contributions become part of Valerie's wonderful haven.

Auxiliary Verbs

Auxiliary verbs, also called helping verbs, never occur without a main verb. An **auxiliary verb** helps the main verb to express tense, voice, or mood, but usually has little meaning of its own. Some examples include *be, do, have, can, might, would, may, will,* and *must*. Two or more verbs combined is called a verb phrase. Verb phrases contain at least one auxiliary verb. Adverbs may appear in the middle of a verb phrase, but they are not part of it.

> Example: We **are** <u>waiting</u> in a long line.
> I **would** have <u>gone</u> with him.
> I **could** hardly <u>wait</u>.

Underline the main verb once. Underline the auxiliary verb(s) twice.

1. The West Highland White Terrier has attained a high degree of popularity as both a loyal pet and a show dog.

2. Before this century, these hardy animals had abounded as working dogs in the Scottish Highlands for over three hundred years.

3. They had earned their livings following fox, badger, and otter for hunters.

4. The ancestors of the breed were known in the past under various names such as Roseneath and Little Skye.

5. The breed was first classified at the annual show of The Scottish Kennel Club in 1904.

6. After 1916, all shows were stopped by World War I.

7. Breeding was prohibited in 1917 and 1918, and no dogs were allowed to be registered.

8. By 1919 breeding had started again, and soon many dogs were registered.

9. A long line of champions has followed.

10. The breed has been described as linty white in color with hard and bristly hair.

11. The Westie should have a long stride, straight shoulders, and a stilted gait.

12. It has been noted for its attentive ears, free, cheerful movement, and high self-esteem.

Name _____   **Verbs**

Linking Verbs

Linking verbs describe conditions instead of actions. They are followed by words that rename or describe the subject. Forms of the verb *to be* are most commonly used as linking verbs, although these forms can also be used as auxiliary verbs in verb phrases. Other forms include *appear, become, feel, grow, look, prove, remain, seem,* and *turn*. These verbs do not function as linking verbs if they do not describe conditions that are followed by a word that renames or describes the subject.

    Example: Carla <u>is</u> my only sister. (linking)
                 Carla's friend <u>is</u> running for governor. (auxiliary)
                 Bob <u>grew</u> sleepy during the long lecture. (linking)
                 Roger <u>grew</u> beautiful roses in his garden. (action)

Look at each underlined verb. If the verb is linking, write L in the blank. If the verb is auxiliary write AUX in the blank. If it is an action verb write ACT in the blank.

_____ 1. Matthew <u>is</u> a really tall fellow.

_____ 2. That puppy <u>is</u> following me again.

_____ 3. The gypsy <u>turned</u> the tarot card.

_____ 4. She <u>turned</u> pale when she saw the ghost.

_____ 5. Marsha <u>became</u> a grandmother at sixty-one.

_____ 6. He <u>was</u> an Elvis look-alike.

_____ 7. Elizabeth <u>felt</u> a fever coming on.

_____ 8. Jennifer <u>felt</u> a bit sheepish.

_____ 9. The maple tree <u>is</u> a good spot for meditating.

_____10. The bee <u>was</u> circling my head.

_____11. His booksack <u>was</u> found in the gym.

_____12. Her purse <u>looked</u> shabby.

_____13. The toddler <u>looked</u> under the bed.

_____14. Mary and Ben <u>remained</u> friends for life.

_____15. The guilty person <u>remained</u> silent.

Principle Parts and Irregular Verbs

The principle parts of a verb are the three forms upon which all tenses are based.

Present	**Past**	**Past Participle** (uses has, have, or had)
love	loved	has, have, or had loved

Many frequently used verbs have principle parts that are irregularly formed.

Present	**Past**	**Past Participle** (uses has, have, or had)
drive	drove	has, have, or had driven

The present form of the verb has been given. Fill in the past and the past participle forms. Use a dictionary to check your work.

Present	**Past**	**Past Participle**
1. forget	_____	_____
2. respond	_____	_____
3. teach	_____	_____
4. forbid	_____	_____
5. sink	_____	_____
6. slip	_____	_____
7. break	_____	_____
8. freeze	_____	_____
9. talk	_____	_____
10. throw	_____	_____
11. choose	_____	_____
12. stroll	_____	_____
13. hear	_____	_____
14. awake	_____	_____
15. be	_____	_____
16. eat	_____	_____
17. allow	_____	_____
18. ride	_____	_____

Principle Parts of Verbs

The principle parts of a verb are the three forms upon which all tenses are based.

| **Present** | **Past** | **Past Participle** (uses has, have, or had) |
| love | loved | has, have, or had loved |

Many frequently used verbs have principle parts that are irregularly formed.

| **Present** | **Past** | **Past Participle** (uses has, have, or had) |
| drive | drove | has, have, or had driven |

Write the verb form that is asked for in each of the following sentences. (P is for past and PP is for past participle). Additional auxiliary verbs may be used.

1. The news of the assassination _____ around the world within minutes of its occurrence.   (PP of *broadcast*)

2. Allison _____ obsessed with losing weight in the past few months.   (PP of *become*)

3. The baby _____ in the middle of the night.
   (P of *cry*)

4. The teller was found after the robbery with his hands _____.
   (P of *bind*)

5. Patricia _____ the perfect dress for her school's Spring Formal.   (PP of *choose*)

6. The fire _____ out of control very quickly.   (P of *burn*)

7. He _____ the metal bar with his bare hands.   (P of *bend*)

8. The principal _____ the unruly student to come to his office after school.   (PP of *instruct*)

9. The aggressive dog _____ the unsuspecting boy on the leg.
   (PP of *bite*)

10. Kristin _____ a large pack of indelible markers.   (P of *buy*)

11. The clock _____ along for hours as Tom tossed and turned.
    (PP of *creep*)

12. The child _____ behind the heavy, brocade curtains.
    (P of *hide*)

Simple Verb Tenses

The tense of the verb shows the time of an action. The **simple present tense** shows that an action takes place now at the same time that it is being described. It is also used to describe habitual action, to tell general truths, and to write about books, movies and other narratives. It can also be used to indicate a time in the future. The **past tense** shows that an action took place at some previous time. The **future tense** shows the action will take place at some time to come.

Examples: The child <u>fills</u> her dog's bowl daily with fresh water. (present, habitual action)
The people <u>elect</u> their government in a democratic society. (present, general truths)
I <u>leave</u> for Costa Rica tomorrow. (present, describing time in future)
He <u>filled</u> the glasses and everyone toasted. (past)
Jenny <u>will fill</u> the garden with bright annuals. (future)

Underline the complete verb. Determine the tense. Write PR for present, PT for past, or F for future on the line provided.

_____ 1. The feisty, young cat scratched the brand new wallpaper with his claws.

_____ 2. I will prune the roses tomorrow.

_____ 3. You know the answer to that question.

_____ 4. Mrs. Schon left the country for several months to live in a warmer climate.

_____ 5. *The Little Prince* by Antoine de Saint-Exupery is an enchanting fable filled

with hidden truths.

_____ 6. Meg will bake sugar cookies with colorful sprinkles for the Christmas party.

_____ 7. Mother gave each of her daughters a cashmere sweater for their birthdays.

_____ 8. Drew yawned enormously.

_____ 9. The new movie features an outstanding cast of talented young actresses.

_____10. In your opinion, is the most exciting city in the United States New York or Los

Angeles?

_____11. The recipe for vegetarian lasagna was on the back of the package of pasta.

_____12. She gave us a shy smile.

_____13. Will you be dining with us this evening?

_____14. How old is the child in this play?

Simple Past Tense

Rewrite each sentence below in the simple past tense.

1. I find that story very amusing.

   _____

2. The bird chirps on my window sill every morning.

   _____

   _____

3. The scissors cut very poorly.

   _____

4. Jan will sell her jewelry at the flea market.

   _____

5. Mother fixes a balanced lunch for each of her children to take to school.

   _____

   _____

6. Sarah will tell a scary tale around the campfire.

   _____

7. Patty always insists on seeing the positive side of a situation.

   _____

   _____

8. Patrick will ride in the Kentucky Derby.

   _____

9. The pages tear easily.

   _____

10. The audience laughs at every line.

   _____

Simple Past Tense

Supply a past tense verb to complete each sentence below.

1. I _____ a mile in six minutes and ten seconds.

2. Esther _____ the silver until it gleamed.

3. You _____ without looking at the keys.

4. Myra _____ a dress of pale blue silk.

5. Mr. Frazier _____ in his favorite old chair.

6. Christopher _____ his science project on Wednesday.

7. Mrs. Temple _____ her money in an old coffee can.

8. Both of us _____ until we fell asleep.

9. Al _____ through the strong current.

10. We _____ to the class about plagiarism.

11. You _____ your stock for ten cents on the dollar.

12. Mr. Blake _____ his holiday in Kansas visiting relatives.

13. None of us _____ fifty dollars from the cash register.

14. The crystal glass _____ on the hard tile floor.

15. Too many of you _____ incredibly fatty food.

16. The ice cream _____ in the heat.

17. Shelley _____ the whole box of pencils all over the floor.

18. Jack and I _____ across the street after dinner.

19. Vicki _____ delectable spinach and oyster soup.

20. Linda _____ her purse on a table in the library.

Simple Present Tense

Supply a present tense verb in each sentence below.

1. The principal _____ my parents very well.

2. We _____ whenever we get the chance.

3. The dog _____ at everything that moves.

4. I _____ the mail every evening.

5. The yacht _____ in a few hours.

6. The bus usually _____ on schedule.

7. The recipe does not _____ enough detail.

8. The door _____ whenever the wind blows.

9. The dictionary _____ more information than just definitions.

10. The play _____ next weekend.

11. The toddler _____ the puppy like her rag doll.

12. The movie _____ a lot of action.

13. The crown _____ not actually made of precious stones.

14. Mary and I _____ the dishes to help his mother.

15. You should _____ to the doctor for an annual checkup.

16. Both of you _____ a lot of money on shoes.

17. Our family _____ a bright red convertible.

18. Madeline _____ pink lipstick.

19. The detective _____ every lead.

20. You two _____ when she appears.

Simple Present Tense

Rewrite each sentence in the simple present tense.

1. Betsy went to the park without me.

   _____

2. Mr. Avery will go to Hong Kong in the spring.

   _____

   _____

3. Sharon ate chocolate quite frequently.

   _____

4. The emergency room staff awaited the unexpected.

   _____

   _____

5. The tutor will help with reducing fractions.

   _____

6. Melody knew the name of that tune.

   _____

7. That lamb will follow her to school every day.

   _____

8. Alex read himself to sleep every night.

   _____

9. To the delight of her fans, the singer will arrive this afternoon.

   _____

   _____

10. Michael loved to paint colorful sunsets.

   _____

Simple Future Tense

Rewrite each sentence in the simple future tense.

1. Valerie bought a new dress to wear to the opera.

   _____

2. The instructor teaches young campers to swim.

   _____

3. I tried very hard to meet the deadline.

   _____

4. The cookies baked in ten minutes.

   _____

5. The star member of the basketball team gets a lot of publicity.

   _____

   _____

6. The photographer took school pictures in October.

   _____

   _____

7. This type of toy breaks easily.

   _____

8. The sculpture was displayed in front of City Hall.

   _____

9. That car was used in the parade.

   _____

10. Roberta appeared on a local television program this week.

   _____

   _____

Simple Future Tense

Rewrite each sentence in the simple future tense.

1. I finished my homework after dinner.

_____

2. The toddler tore the pretty picture book.

_____

3. The plane departs at twelve noon.

_____

4. Alexander had to take another aspirin.

_____

5. The travel agent held the reservation for twenty-four hours.

_____

_____

6. The president gave a televised speech on the economy.

_____

_____

7. Barbara called me about the matter.

_____

8. Margaret visited Ireland in October.

_____

9. The Smith family got to skate at the rink in Central Park.

_____

_____

10. Did you tell me the whole truth?

_____

Name _____

Past Perfect Tense

The **past perfect tense** describes an event in the past in relation to another event in the past. It shows that an action was completed before another action in the past, or completed before a definite time. The past perfect tense uses *had* and the past participle form of the main verb.

Example: She <u>had jogged</u> for twenty minutes before she began to feel faint.
The Smiths <u>had been married</u> for ten years before their first child was born.

Fill in the blank using the past perfect form of the verb.

1. (learn) During the summer vacation Roger _____ wilderness survival skills.

2. (eat) The children _____ pizza after three hours of bowling.

3. (consider) I acted before I _____ the consequences.

4. (finish) Beth _____ reading before the rest of us started.

5. (drive) Patricia _____ over three hundred miles yesterday.

6. (sing) Myra _____ that aria several times in her career.

7. (take) The rehearsal _____ more time than expected.

8. (slip) Her ring _____ from her finger when she washed her hands.

9. (howl) The wind _____ all through the night.

10. (choose) They _____ a place for the honeymoon before they called off their wedding.

11. (look) His candidacy for mayor _____ good until the scandal was publicized.

12. (love) The benevolent king _____ his loyal subjects for many years.

Past Perfect Tense

Create a sentence using the past perfect tense of each given verb.

1. **(kiss)** _____

_____

2. **(announce)** _____

_____

3. **(break)** _____

_____

4. **(challenge)** _____

_____

5. **(release)** _____

_____

6. **(wear)** _____

_____

7. **(tear)** _____

_____

8. **(study)** _____

_____

9. **(take)** _____

_____

10. **(bark)** _____

_____

Present Perfect Tense

The **present perfect tense** describes an event that started in the past and continues to be the same in the present. It uses either *has* or *have* plus the past participle form of the verb.

> Example :   He <u>has known</u> her for ten years.
> We <u>have seen</u> the play several times.

Write the present perfect form of the verb in each blank.

1. (frighten) That old scarecrow _____ crows from the cornfield for years.

2. (bake) Melanie's mother _____ six dozen cookies for the fund raiser.

3. (trap) The cat _____ the mouse in the corner.

4. (visit) Those volunteers _____ the nursing home every Sunday.

5. (buy) I _____ a new notebook for biology.

6. (read) John _____ Treasure Island more than once.

7. (hold) I _____ your heavy suitcase for hours.

8. (write) Pamela _____ a letter to the president.

9. (work) Cedric _____ on the computer all afternoon.

10. (bring) Who _____ a donation for the United Way?

11. (draw) Ms. Louis _____ interesting caricatures for years.

12. (fall) The picture _____ from the wall again.

13. (is) There _____ a gloomy atmosphere around here all afternoon.

14. (follow) Penny _____ the rules.

15. (run) Your time _____ out.

Present Perfect Tense

Read each sentence then underline the verb. Write in the blank if the tense is simple present (PR), simple past (PT), or simple future (F). Rewrite the sentence in the present perfect tense.

_____ 1. The mahogany table was scratched. _____

_____

_____ 2. Mr. Anderson will change jobs this year. _____

_____

_____ 3. The kicker scored nine points. _____

_____

_____ 4. Marcia often cries crocodile tears. _____

_____

_____ 5. Emily dreamed of finding pirate's loot. _____

_____

_____ 6. That company will send me a sample of its product. _____

_____

_____ 7. Jennifer left a message on the answer phone. _____

_____

_____ 8. Mr. Moore worked for that firm for years. _____

_____

_____ 9. They will spend years on that research project. _____

_____

_____10. Chris always knows the latest gossip. _____

_____

Future Perfect Tense

The **future perfect tense** shows that an action will happen after something else in the future. It uses *will* (or *shall* with first person), *has* or *have*, and the past participle form of the verb.

> Example: He <u>will have surrendered</u> by that time.
> I <u>will have completed</u> the painting by Tuesday.

Supply a future perfect tense verb to complete each sentence below.

1. I _____ you by twelve o'clock.

2. The exam grades _____ on the classroom door
   for two hours before the building closes.

3. My father _____ a new van in the spring.

4. Beth's mother _____ all of the costumes for the play by
   the afternoon of dress rehearsal.

5. The company _____ a profit for the first time this year.

6. You _____ by the time he gets here.

7. I _____ my new jeans for two days when I wash them.

8. Jane _____ her room before the week ends.

9. Mr. Sullivan's friends _____ him a surprise
   birthday party the Saturday before his fiftieth birthday.

10. The mallard ducks _____ to this area by the time winter
    comes.

Future Perfect Tense

Look at the given verb. Create a sentence in the future perfect tense using each verb.

1. (learn)_____

_____

2. (make)_____

_____

3. (see)_____

_____

4. (try)_____

_____

5. (hop)_____

_____

6. (throw)_____

_____

7. (write)_____

_____

8. (play)_____

_____

9. (forget)_____

_____

10. (bought)_____

_____

Progressive Form of a Verb

The **progressive form** of a verb indicates continuous or habitual action, or an event in progress. It is formed by adding *-ing* to a main verb (the present participle) that is preceded by an auxiliary verb.

Example:		simple	progressive
	present:	tell	is telling
	past:	told	was telling
	future:	will tell	will be telling

Underline the simple verb in each sentence. Rewrite each simple verb in the progressive form.

1. The puppy digs holes in the back yard.

   _____

2. The airlines will start a fare war this month.

   _____

3. Mr. Allen rewards his children for good report cards.

   _____

   _____

4. The robber fled the scene of the crime.

   _____

5. The children sell lemonade in the summer to make money.

   _____

   _____

6. His words broke my heart.

   _____

7. The package arrives tomorrow.

   _____

8. The mothers will sew all of the costumes for the class play.

   _____

   _____

Verb Tense Review

Underline the complete verb in each sentence. Select the letter of the verb tense it uses and write it on the line provided.

A) simple present   D) present perfect   G) present progressive
B) simple past   E) past perfect   H) past progressive
C) simple future   F) future perfect   I) future progressive

_____ 1. Patricia has found the treasure map.

_____ 2. The weather was hot and humid.

_____ 3. Mr. Mitchell has finally discovered the solution to his problem.

_____ 4. Will you be attending the graduation ceremony?

_____ 5. The robber was running from the scene of the crime.

_____ 6. I am responsible for the entire matter.

_____ 7. The dancers froze at that instant.

_____ 8. I will give serious thought to your proposal.

_____ 9. Find my car keys, please.

_____10. The computer was not turned off all night.

_____11. I was trying to reach you on your car phone this afternoon.

_____12. Many bald eagles have been spotted in Montana lately.

_____13. Polly has a peanut butter and banana sandwich for lunch.

_____14. That calendar is out-of-date.

_____15. You are trying your best.

Verb Tense Review

Underline the complete verb in each sentence. Write its tense on the line provided.

A) simple present   D) present perfect   G) present progressive
B) simple past   E) past perfect   H) past progressive
C) simple future   F) future perfect   I) future progressive

Change the sentence to the tense requested and make any adjustments necessary.

Example: He <u>ran</u> to the store.   He <u>was running</u> to the store.
simple past   *past progressive*

_____ 1. Ms. Wilson is running for lieutenant governor. (simple future)

_____

_____ 2. I get tired easily. (present progressive)

_____

_____ 3. The decision was made in haste. (present perfect)

_____

_____ 4. Max drove all day. (future progressive)

_____

_____ 5. The baby is crying in her crib. (past progressive)

_____

_____ 6. Milly tells the truth. (past perfect)

_____

_____ 7. Dan has read that novel. (past)

_____

_____ 8. Wendell taped the program. (future perfect)

_____

_____ 9. Jane will change her mind. (simple past)

_____

_____10. We danced all night. (future perfect)

_____

Verb Tense Review

Underline the complete verb in each sentence. Write its tense on the line provided.

A) simple present   D) present perfect   G) present progressive
B) simple past   E) past perfect   H) past progressive
C) simple future   F) future perfect   I) future progressive

Change the sentence to the tense requested and make any adjustments necessary.

Example: He <u>ran</u> to the store.   He <u>was running</u> to the store.
             simple past   *past progressive*

_____ 1. Jane will be attending the conference. (simple future)

_____

_____ 2. Sam found the history test difficult. (present progressive)

_____

_____ 3. Marius fell madly in love with Cosette. (future perfect)

_____

_____ 4. Ralph had known Mrs. Smith for years. (present perfect)

_____

_____ 5. He located his fishing tackle box in the garage. (past perfect)

_____

_____ 6. Frank will find the old trunk in his aunt's attic. (simple past)

_____

_____ 7. It will take a lot of time to polish the silver. (simple present)

_____

_____ 8. George was collecting for the charity. (simple past)

_____

_____ 9. The letter arrived three days late. (future progressive)

_____

_____10. I had already gone to that movie. (future perfect)

_____

Gerunds

A **gerund** is a verb that is used as a noun. It uses the *-ing* verb ending. Like verbs, gerunds name actions or conditions. Like nouns, gerunds function as the subject, direct object, predicate nominative, or object of the preposition. A gerund can stand alone, or it can be part of a gerund phrase.

Example: Dame Van Winkle was <u>nagging</u> her husband, Rip. (verb)
Dame Van Winkle's <u>nagging</u> made Rip's life miserable. (gerund as S)
Rip Van Winkle hated his wife's <u>nagging</u>. (gerund as DO)
The cause of Rip's discontent was his wife's <u>nagging</u>. (gerund as PN)
Rip's life from the constant <u>nagging</u> was unbearable. (gerund as OP)

Underline the gerund. Choose its function in the sentence from the following: S for subject, DO for direct object, PN for predicate nominative, or OP for object of the preposition. If there is no gerund in the sentence, write NONE.

_____ 1. **Studying preoccupied Mary during the week of final exams.**

_____ 2. **Peter loves sailing on his yacht with his friends and family.**

_____ 3. **Smoking contributed to his serious heart condition.**

_____ 4. **Playing is the work of young children.**

_____ 5. **My favorite form of exercise is jogging.**

_____ 6. **Natalie enjoys driving her mother's four wheel drive utility vehicle.**

_____ 7. **Diving is dangerous in this shallow lake.**

_____ 8. **Acting is her favorite extracurricular activity.**

_____ 9. **An ineffective method of studying is simply memorizing.**

_____ 10. **He was preoccupied with thoughts about dying.**

_____ 11. **Whining won't get you your way.**

_____ 12. **Stretching is important after exercise.**

_____ 13. **Jasmine couldn't cope with losing.**

_____ 14. **Rebecca got in trouble, as usual, for talking with her large circle of friends.**

_____ 15. **Daisy will be collecting food items for Thanksgiving baskets for the poor this week.**

Limiting and Descriptive Adjectives

An **adjective** modifies a noun (or pronoun). There are several kinds. **Descriptive adjectives** describe a noun by making the meaning more precise. There are also two kinds of **limiting adjectives** called *definite* and *indefinite* articles. The definite article *the* specifies a particular noun. The indefinite articles *a* and *an* generalize the noun.

> Example: <u>shabby</u> couch (descriptive)
> <u>honest</u> priest (descriptive)
> <u>the</u> truth (limiting)
> <u>a</u> sign (limiting and used before words beginning with a consonant sound)
> <u>an</u> apple (limiting and used before words beginning with a vowel sound)

Underline each descriptive or limiting adjective. Classify it as descriptive (D) or limiting (L).

1. Every year many curious visitors visit Manhattan to see what the city is really like.

2. There are good reasons why so many fall in love with this bustling metropolis.

3. One special moment is when the house lights dim at the Metropolitan Opera and the sparkling chandeliers ascend into the ceiling.

4. The golden statue of Prometheus in Rockefeller Center is also an enthralling sight.

5. The lofty rows of skyscrapers which make up the familiar skyline are another lure for the first-time tourist.

6. Could one look up at the Empire State Building without movie memories of the giant ape King Kong?

7. A leisurely stroll down the famous Mulberry Street in Little Italy will fill the visitor's senses with delectable sights and smells.

8. The colossal Statue of Liberty is a definite challenge to climb.

9. This beautiful statue attracts a multitude of tourists.

10. Tourists always make time to walk in that incredible green oasis in the middle of Manhattan called Central Park.

Name _____

Comparison of Adjectives

An adjective that compares the qualities of one noun or pronoun to another (*clearer* or *more athletic*) uses the **comparative** form. An adjective that compares the qualities of more than two nouns or pronouns (*oldest* or *most dangerous*) uses the **superlative** form. Most adjectives with one syllable form their comparatives by adding *-er* and their superlative by adding *-est*. Some adjectives with two syllables only add *more* for the comparative and *most* for the superlative. Some can use either form (*more, most, -er,* or *-est*). You may need to consult the dictionary to be sure that you are using the correct form. Adjectives containing three or more syllables generally use *more* or *most*.

Example:	Adjective	Comparative form	Superlative
(1 syllable)	fast	faster	fastest
(2 syllables)	active	more active	most active
(2 syllables)	friendly	friendlier	friendliest
	friendly	more friendly	most friendly
(3 syllables)	efficient	more efficient	most efficient

Fill in the comparative and superlative forms of the adjectives listed below.

Adjective	Comparative Form	Superlative Form
1. adequate	_____	_____
2. loud	_____	_____
3. narrow	_____	_____
4. busy	_____	_____
5. green	_____	_____
6. cold	_____	_____
7. sympathetic	_____	_____
8. agreeable	_____	_____
9. prosperous	_____	_____
10. selfish	_____	_____
11. greedy	_____	_____
12. kind	_____	_____
13. difficult	_____	_____
14. fantastic	_____	_____

Comparison of Adjectives

Fill in the blank with the correct form of the adjective.

1. (phony) The counterfeit dollar bill looked _____ than the ten dollar bill.

2. (sharp) This pencil is _____ than that one.

3. (straight) Maggie could draw the _____ lines in her class.

4. (expensive) He always buys the _____ shoes in the store.

5. (cold) He gave me the _____ look that I ever received.

6. (convenient) This library is the _____ one in town for the students.

7. (serious) She has always been _____ than her sister.

8. (valuable) The diamond brooch is _____ than the ruby ring.

9. (distinguished) Meghan delivered the _____ speech in her grade.

10. (eager) Sally is _____ to attend the dance than Beulah.

11. (wise) The teacher's advice was _____ than the dropout's.

12. (cold) This has been the _____ winter in years.

13. (helpful) Ms. Hopkins is _____ than Mr. Bennet.

14. (bright) Venus is the _____ star in the sky.

15. (colorful) That is the _____ poster in the campaign.

Pronouns as Adjectives

Pronouns take the place of nouns. Adjectives describe nouns or pronouns. The same word can function as an adjective or pronoun depending on its use in the sentence.

Example: <u>That</u> is really expensive. (pronoun)
<u>That</u> dress is really expensive. (adjective-modifies dress)
<u>Some</u> of you can come. (pronoun)
<u>Some</u> students are coming with us. (adjective-modifies students)

Underline the pronoun in each sentence. Identify the function of each as P (pronoun) or A (adjective). For this exercise, skip the limiting adjectives (articles) *a, an*, and *the* when you indentify adjectives.

_____ 1. This is my friend, Rosilee.

_____ 2. Bruce will buy whichever is left.

_____ 3. Madeline can buy any car she wants.

_____ 4. Was Bob interested in any of them?

_____ 5. This is my friend, Albert.

_____ 6. Betty ate some of these apples.

_____ 7. Those girls read *Jane Eyre* in the fall.

_____ 8. Each one found a seat.

_____ 9. Those weren't on the shelf.

_____10. Cheryl doesn't want any.

_____11. Any of these are working.

_____12. <u>That</u> responsibility is yours.

Write four of your own sentences. Use *most* and *these* as both adjectives and pronouns.

1. _____

2. _____

3. _____

4. _____

Comparison of Adverbs

An **adverb** identifies the word that it modifies (verb, adjective or adverb) as having certain qualities. An adverb that compares two things uses the **comparative** form. An adverb that compares
the qualities of more than two things uses the **superlative** form. Most adverbs with one syllable
form their comparatives by adding -er and their superlatives by adding -est. Some adverbs with
two syllables only add more for the comparative and most for the superlative. Some can use
either form (more/most or -er/-est). You may need to consult the dictionary to be sure that you
are using the correct form. Adverbs containing three or more syllables generally use only more
or most as well as less or least.

Example:	Positive	Comparative	Superlative
(1 syllable)	soon	sooner	soonest
(2 syllables)	often	more often	most often
(2 syllables)	friendly	friendlier	friendliest
	friendly	more friendly	most friendly
(3 syllables)	beautifully	more beautifully	most beautifully

Fill in the comparative and superlative forms.

Positive	Comparative Form	Superlative Form
1. early		
2. highly		
3. deep		
4. bravely		
5. gracefully		
6. quickly		
7. adequately		
8. hard		
9. obviously		
10. neatly		
11. high		
12. soon		
13. quietly		

Name _____

Comparison of Adverbs

Fill in the blank with the correct comparative or superlative form of the adverb.

1. **(high)** Lorraine can jump _____ than any of the competitors.

2. **(fairly)** My math teacher grades _____ than my science teacher.

3. **(early)** Seven o'clock in the morning is the _____ time that you can arrive at school.

4. **(slowly)** Randolph does his homework _____ than Rudy.

5. **(seriously)** Although everyone on the bus was injured, the people in the rear were injured _____.

6. **(commonly)** The _____ found food at American barbecues is the hamburger.

7. **(frequently)** Trang needs to visit the dentist _____ than she does.

8. **(often)** Albert jogs _____ at daybreak than at sunset.

9. **(thoroughly)** We searched _____ the second time.

10. **(sensibly)** Joy eats _____ than her brother.

11. **(steadily)** Blake steered the boat _____ after the wind and rain subsided.

12. **(soon)** I hope that you arrive _____ than my blind date.

13. **(smoothly)** My new pen writes _____ than my old one.

14. **(gracefully)** Michelle danced the _____ of all the swans in *Swan Lake*.

15. **(fast)** Beth ran _____ of all.

Name _____   **Comparisons**

Comparison of Irregular Adjectives and Adverbs

Some commonly used adjectives and adverbs are compared irregularly.

Example:

positive	comparative	superlative
bad (adj)	worse	worst
badly (adv)	worse	worst

Look at the irregular comparative. Write the comparative and superlative form.

Positive	Comparative	Superlative
1. little	_____	_____
2. much	_____	_____
3. ill	_____	_____
4. many	_____	_____
5. well	_____	_____
6. far	_____	_____
7. good	_____	_____

Complete each sentence using the correct comparative form of the adjective or adverb.

1. (well) I feel _____ than I did yesterday.

2. (many) She received the _____ applause at Saturday's performance.

3. (little) He received _____ computer training than I had.

4. (old) Aunt Marie was the _____ person at the party.

5. (badly) Malachi performed _____ in the class on the pop quiz.

6. (far) Joy lives the _____ from school of all of her classmates.

© Carson-Dellosa CD-3744   49

Identifying Prepositions and Prepositional Phrases

Prepositions connect nouns and pronouns to other words in a sentence and show their relationship. They never stand alone. They introduce a prepositional phrase that contains a noun or pronoun and its modifiers. Prepositional phrases do not include verbs.

Example: She found the spoon _under_ the kitchen table.
It was the morning _before_ the wedding.
We saw a blue bird _in the sycamore tree_.

Fill in the blank with a preposition. Underline the phrase it introduces.

1. Charlotte Brontë, the author of _Jane Eyre_ lived _____ 1816 to 1855.

2. Charlotte was the eldest _____ the four Bronte sisters.

3. _____ their childhood, Charlotte and her sister Emily attended a school that both girls hated because _____ its inhumane treatment _____ the students.

4. Charlotte wrote a scathing account _____ this heartless school _____ her book, _Jane Eyre_.

5. _____ 1842 Charlotte went _____ Brussels.

6. She worked _____ a while _____ a governess there.

7. Her heroine Jane also spent most _____ her time _____ a governess.

8. Charlotte returned home soon _____ Brussels.

9. She was needed desperately _____ her blind father, alcoholic brother, and gravely ill sisters.

10. The sisters tried publishing a book _____ poems, but were unsuccessful.

11. The sisters then returned _____ writing fiction, and each produced a novel.

12. Charlotte's first book, _The Professor_, was flatly and coldly refused _____ the publishers.

13. Her next novel, _Jane Eyre_, was very successful; _____ it she received much fame and praise.

Identifying Prepositions and Prepositional Phrases

Extend each sentence by adding a preposition or a prepositional phrase.

1. **Meghan walked her dog** _____.

2. **The sparrow flew** _____.

3. **The ball bounced** _____.

4. **His glasses fell** _____.

5. **Elizabeth stared** _____.

6. **The loot was found** _____.

7. **The house** _____ **was charming.**

8. **The girl** _____ **came alone.**

9. **Irene baked cookies** _____.

10. **A chattering squirrel ran** _____.

11. **The barge plowed** _____.

12. **Carla won a trip** _____.

13. **The Green family lives** _____.

14. **We were hungry** _____ **that we prepared the feast.**

15. **The bouquet** _____ **was a thoughtful gift.**

16. **The map** _____ **was not up-to-date.**

17. **The face** _____ **looked tired.**

18. **The roses** _____ **were stunning in full bloom.**

19. **The boys came** _____ **when it started raining.**

20. **Our parade will begin** _____.

Identifying Prepositions and Prepositional Phrases

Fill in the blank with a preposition. Underline the phrase it introduces.

1. Mr. Post is riding the Orient Express _____ Paris _____ Venice.

2. Bob was _____ the movie theater when the fire started.

3. The capital _____ Maine is Augusta.

4. That cantankerous black cat lives _____ this street.

5. The remote was hidden _____ the sofa cushion.

6. The makeup artist turned the actor _____ a monster.

7. We left the disappointing performance _____ the intermission.

8. A crowd gathered _____ the scene _____ the accident.

9. Ralph has been anxiously waiting all week _____ that letter.

10. The painting fell _____ the wall _____ no apparent reason.

11. The content kitten slept _____ its mother.

12. The fireworks will begin _____ dark.

13. The invitation went _____ the wrong address.

14. The ball rolled _____ the bushes.

15. She climbed _____ the steep stone stairs _____ the castle.

16. The dog waited _____ his master _____ dusk every evening.

17. A really pretty girl sat _____ Andy _____ the movies.

18. The boy _____ my class won the election.

19. Sylvia and her mother set flowers _____ the new dining room table.

20. _____ the storm, we picked up branches and raked fallen leaves.

Coordinating Conjunctions

Conjunctions join words or groups of words. One kind of conjunction is the **coordinating conjunction.** Coordinating conjunctions connect single words, phrases (combinations of words that go together within sentences) and clauses (word combinations containing a subject and predicate) that are of the same importance or rank. The most common ones are *and*, *but*, and *or*.

> Example: The children feasted on cookies <u>and</u> milk. (joins words)
> The kids asked me to come <u>and</u> join them. (joins phrases)
> I can go, <u>but</u> you can't. (joins clauses or simple sentences)

Read each sentence. Supply an appropriate coordinating conjunction. Write on the line if it joins words (W), phrases (P), or clauses/simple sentences (C).

_____ 1. **Roses need good drainage, _____ their leaves will turn yellow.**

_____ 2. **Eugene considered the punishment cruel _____ unusual.**

_____ 3. **It is possible _____ not very likely.**

_____ 4. **We waited in the terminal for hours, _____ our connection didn't ever arrive.**

_____ 5. **He was born and raised in Ohio, _____ now lives in New York.**

_____ 6. **Sue decides on the itinerary, _____ Joe makes the travel arrangements.**

_____ 7. **Sam has been driving _____ making sales calls for weeks.**

_____ 8. **I couldn't go, _____ Janet could.**

_____ 9. **He gladly received her hugs _____ kisses.**

_____10. **Carmen _____ Mimi won't admit their ages.**

_____11. **Marcus _____ Rudolpho won't admit their weights.**

_____12. **I don't eat fat _____ sugar.**

_____13. **Alexander looked everywhere, _____ the book had vanished.**

_____14. **The homeless shelter needs donations of food _____ clothing.**

53

Correlative Conjunctions

Conjunctions join words or groups of words. **Correlative conjunctions** are paired connective words that link single words, phrases (combinations of words that go together within sentences), and clauses (word combinations containing subjects and predicates). The correlative conjunctions are: *both...and, neither...nor, whether...or, either...or, not only...but* (or *but also*).

    Examples: She has met <u>neither</u> Polly <u>nor</u> Renee. (joins words)
                   She can prepare <u>either</u> a detailed outline <u>or</u> a structured overview. (joins phrases)
                   I don't know <u>whether</u> Peter will go <u>or</u> Jack will. (joins clauses)

Read each sentence and supply the appropriate correlative conjunctions in the blanks. Write in the blank if the correlative conjunctions join words (W), phrases (P) or clauses (C).

_____ 1. You will need _____ pencil _____ paper.

_____ 2. The toddler drinks _____ milk _____ apple juice.

_____ 3. Blake's exercise program includes _____ aerobic workouts

                   _____ weight training.

_____ 4. _____ cookies _____ potato chips should
                   appear so regularly in your lunch box.

_____ 5. He is guilty of _____ pickpocketing _____ burglary.

_____ 6. _____ did he take my wallet _____ my television.

_____ 7. You must decide _____ to ask Anne _____ Maria.

_____ 8. _____ help me _____ leave me alone.

_____ 9. _____ Jim _____ Brian asked Krystal to dance.

_____10. I can't decide _____ I want to see a movie, _____
                   or eat dinner.

_____11. The menu includes _____ Cajun _____ French food.

_____12. _____ come with me, _____ I'll go alone.

Subordinating Conjunctions

Subordinating conjunctions connect clauses and indicate that one of the two clauses is more important to the basic meaning of the sentence. The less important (dependent) clause is introduced by the subordinating conjunction and gives additional meaning to the main clause. There are many subordinating conjunctions. Some of the most common include *after, although, as, because, before, if, since, unless, whatever, when, whenever, where, wherever,* and *while.* Subordinating conjunctions can appear in the beginning or in the middle of a sentence.

Example: (Until) you finish your homework, don't turn on the television.

Barbara will decorate for the party (while) I wrap the presents.

Circle the subordinating conjunction. Underline the dependent clause that it introduces.

1. If you are a serious traveler, you should carry the right gear.

2. Use an all-purpose, water resistant camera with a zoom lens when you take pictures.

3. Although you may not know the uses for all of its 31 tools, bring along a Swiss army knife.

4. If your dog must come, bring a collapsible dog bowl with a waterproof, nylon lining.

5. Carry a fold-up bag inside your luggage when you plan to bring home a lot of souvenirs.

6. Unless you know that the weather will be consistently cold, carry a convertible jacket with removable sleeves.

7. There are also cotton pants with zip-off legs if you find yourself warm enough to be in shorts.

8. Since health and safety are always considerations, carry an emergency first aid kit.

9. If you are concerned about foreign fire safety codes, bring along your own lightweight, battery-powered smoke alarm.

10. Because you do not always find your bare feet in the most sanitary of places, carry skid-resistant rubber shoes with mesh netting uppers.

Using Interjections

Interjections express some emotion and have no grammatical connection to the sentence. They can be followed by a comma or an exclamation point. Some commonly used interjections include: *Oh, Great, Wow, Ouch, Hey, Please,* and *No.*

Example: <u>Oh</u>, so there you are!
            <u>Great</u>! I left my umbrella at home.

Add an interjection to each sentence.

1. _____! Do not interrupt the speaker.

2. _____, what a wonderful time we had on safari!

3. _____, this is a fabulous pasta primavera.

4. _____, what a fabulous experience for the students!

5. _____! So you have finally decided to go.

6. _____, what an incredibly rude thing to say!

7. _____, I can't take it anymore.

8. _____, you look great in those high heels!

9. _____! The police are coming.

10. _____, the earth is shaking!

11. _____, get out of here!

12. _____, I love this class!

13. _____! Stop blaring that radio.

14. _____! Come help me.

15. _____, I need more time!

Parts of Speech Review

Identify the part of speech of each underlined word in the paragraphs that follow. Write the part of speech on the numbered line. Use the following abbreviations:

noun (**N**)   adjective (**ADJ**)   pronoun (**P**)   conjunction (**C**)
verb (**V**)   adverb (**ADV**)   preposition (**PREP**)   interjection (**IN**)

Mont-St-Michel

Mont-St-Michel dominates the white beaches <u>between</u> the provinces of <u>Normandy</u> and
₁   ₂

Brittany in France. If you <u>have</u> the opportunity to view Mont-St-Michel as <u>it</u> emerges from
₃   ₄

the ocean at high tide, you <u>will</u> agree that it is a <u>truly</u> unforgettable experience. It is such
₅   ₆

an <u>architectural</u> wonder that it has often been called "Marvel of the West."
₇

The legend says that in the <u>eighth</u> century, Archangel St. Michael appeared to a <u>local</u>
₈   ₉

bishop and ordered <u>him</u> to build a chapel on top of a 258 foot high <u>mount</u>. An abbey
₁₀   ₁₁

quickly followed, <u>which</u> in order to accommodate the increasing number <u>of</u> pilgrims from
₁₂   ₁₃

all over Europe, was constantly embellished <u>and</u> enlarged with new constructions, some
₁₄

times built on top of each <u>other</u>.
₁₅

The <u>result</u> of all this construction is one of <u>medieval</u> Europe's masterpieces. <u>Indeed</u>, it
₁₆   ₁₇   ₁₈

is <u>surely</u> <u>one</u> of the world's great masterpieces.
₁₉   ₂₀

1. ____	6. ____	11. ____	16. ____
2. ____	7. ____	12. ____	17. ____
3. ____	8. ____	13. ____	18. ____
4. ____	9. ____	14. ____	19. ____
5. ____	10. ____	15. ____	20. ____

Parts of Speech Review

Identify the part of speech of each underlined word in the paragraphs that follow. Write the part of speech on the numbered line. Use the following abbreviations:

noun (**N**)   adjective (**ADJ**)   pronoun (**P**)   conjunction (**C**)
verb (**V**)   adverb (**ADV**)   preposition (**PREP**)   interjection (**IN**)

Demeter and Persephone

The story of Demeter and Persephone was <u>first</u> <u>told</u> by Homer <u>in</u> a Greek poem dating
                                1 2   3

back to the seventh <u>century</u>. It tells the tragic tale of Demeter, the goddess of the <u>harvest</u>,
                4   5

and her <u>daughter</u>, Persephone.
        6

One day Persephone was on Earth picking flowers. Suddenly the ground opened up
and she was taken hostage by Hades, the lord of the underworld.

Demeter could not get <u>over</u> her grief. The year was <u>dreadful</u> for <u>mankind</u> all over the
                          7   8   9

Earth <u>because</u> Demeter <u>allowed</u> nothing to grow. When it became <u>apparent</u> that all
      10   11   12

mankind would <u>die</u> of famine, Zeus, the king of the gods, <u>decided</u> to intervene.
          13   14

Zeus sent <u>his</u> messenger Hermes down to the kingdom of the dead to secure the
         15

<u>release</u> of Persephone. Hades <u>reluctantly</u> agreed to release <u>her</u> only if she would return
16   17   18

to him for four months every year. This length of time was decided upon because she
had eaten four <u>pomegranate</u> seeds while in captivity, and this act bound her to Hades for
                  19

eternity.

Demeter was overjoyed to see her daughter. The Earth became fertile again. But
every year when Persephone returned to her husband Hades, Demeter turned the earth

cold and <u>barren</u> once more.
      20

1. _____	6. _____	11. _____	16. _____
2. _____	7. _____	12. _____	17. _____
3. _____	8. _____	13. _____	18. _____
4. _____	9. _____	14. _____	19. _____
5. _____	10. _____	15. _____	20. _____

Simple Subject and Simple Predicate

In order to be a sentence (or complete thought), two elements are necessary: a **subject** (the person, place, or thing spoken about) and a **predicate** (says something about the person, place, or thing). The **simple subject** (SS) is the key word that the sentence is about. The **simple predicate** (SP) is the verb (action or linking) that describes the action of the subject or some condition about the subject. Modifiers (including adjectives, adverbs, and prepositional phrases) are not included in the simple subject or simple predicate.

> Example: • key words only:
> > <u>Roger</u> / <u>returned</u>.
> > SS   SP
> • with modifiers:
> > Jubilant <u>Roger</u> / <u>returned</u> in triumph.
> >   SS   SP
> • with modifiers and an object of the action verb:
> > Jubilant <u>Roger</u> / quickly <u>returned</u> the stolen masterpiece to the museum.
> >   SS   SP
> • with modifiers and a condition about the subject following the linking verb:
> > <u>Roger</u> / <u>was</u> jubilant about the recovery of the masterpiece.
> > SS   SP

Underline the simple subject. Circle the simple predicate.

1. **A great way to get to Vancouver, British Columbia is by train.**

2. **The train rumbles though spectacular transcontinental scenery.**

3. **Riders cross the Rockies, the Canadian prairies, and the lake-strewn Canadian Shield.**

4. **Train passengers see almost nothing of the cities and towns on the way.**

5. **Instead they see hazy rivers, ridges thick with evergreens, and assorted, pastoral landscapes.**

6. **The Canadian Rockies route through Banff and Lake Louise is probably the most striking.**

7. **Spiral tunnels twist and climb through the mountains.**

8. **Soon Calgary comes into view.**

9. **It is followed by two days of nothing but prairie.**

10. **The Canadian Shield follows the prairie with its hundreds of miles of rock, birch, aspen, and lakes.**

Simple Subject and Simple Predicate

Add the sentence part (subject or predicate) that is missing. Underline the simple subject and circle the simple predicate.

1. The gloomy weather _____.

2. _____ felt good on his parched tongue.

3. The long canoe ride _____.

4. The cuckoo clock _____.

5. _____ sat on a bench in the school yard.

6. _____ burst into laughter at the sight.

7. The stuffed picnic basket _____.

8. _____ will be used for improvements to the school library.

9. Her gigantic purse _____.

10. The sensitive artist _____.

11. _____ will be held in the middle of July.

12. The reason for the error _____.

13. _____ felt very hot to the touch.

14. The torn photograph _____.

15. The aerobic workout _____.

16. _____ was found behind the gym.

17. The memory in his computer _____.

18. The veal stew _____.

19. _____ could be found in the dictionary.

20. _____ wanted to carry the flag.

Compound Subjects

The **subject** answers the question "Who?" or "What?" In some sentences there are two or more nouns that serve as the subject of the same verb.

Example: <u>Mabel</u> and <u>Ben</u> wrote their book reports together.
The tall <u>girl</u> and the freckle-faced <u>boy</u> were finalists in the essay contest.

Underline the nouns for each compound subject.

1. The computer and the printer were ruined in the flood.

2. The white roses, red and yellow columbine, and the lacy fern made a pretty bouquet.

3. Five pens, two three-pocket notebooks, and one pair of scissors were on her school supply list.

4. Oregano, parsley, and rosemary are easy herbs to grow in your garden.

5. Zucchini and asparagus are Manuel's favorite vegetables.

6. Melissa and Shelley disliked the movie enough to leave in the middle.

7. *The Negro Speaks of Rivers* and *Mother to Son* are great poems by Langston Hughes.

8. The dinghy and the sailboat belong to my uncle.

9. The heavy traffic and the summer heat made Allen tense and uncomfortable.

10. The landscape and the portrait will be hung in the parlor.

11. More memory and a larger monitor are needed to upgrade my computer.

12. My collie and the cat next door are great friends.

13. Samuel and his sister are often late for school.

14. The script and the schedule were not in Lyla's briefcase.

15. Mrs. Finley and her black poodle are often seen at local dog shows.

Compound Predicate

A sentence has a **compound predicate** if there are two or more verbs that each have the same subject.

Example: We <u>ate</u> and <u>drank</u> until we were full.
                    (The subject of both verbs is *We*)
             The watch and the ring <u>cost</u> a lot, but <u>were worth</u> the money.
                    (The subject of both verbs is *watch* and *ring*)

Underline the verbs. Write S on the line if it is a simple sentence (the verbs have the same subject).

_____ 1. She led and we followed.

_____ 2. The spoiled child cried and cried for more candy.

_____ 3. The photographer framed and shot a perfect picture.

_____ 4. Sal will wash and dry the dishes.

_____ 5. We heard a crash, and a scream followed.

_____ 6. The rain poured and the wind roared.

_____ 7. Faith danced and sang to the music.

_____ 8. Melissa and Bert found the purse and returned it.

_____ 9. The large dog slobbered and jumped all over me.

_____10. We prune and water the garden twice a week.

_____11. Patrick mopped and swept the floor.

_____12. John and his sister hurried to the counter and bought two tickets.

_____13. Patty washed and dried her pretty auburn hair.

_____14. Don't slip and slide on the wet floor.

_____15. I tried studying but fell asleep.

Compound Predicate

Rewrite each simple sentence with a compound predicate. Remember that both verbs must accompany the same subject for the sentence to be simple.

Example: We <u>sat</u> on the sofa.   We <u>sat</u> and <u>talked</u> on the sofa.
           I <u>felt</u> sorry for her.   I <u>felt</u> sorry for her and <u>forgave</u> her.

1. **The children played in the park.**

   _____

2. **The brothers were arguing in view of everyone.**

   _____

3. **The driver grew sleepy.**

   _____

4. **The class painted with watercolors.**

   _____

5. **The girls watched videos at the slumber party.**

   _____

6. **The talented girl could sing beautifully.**

   _____

7. **The fire started in the attic.**

   _____

8. **Sam found a wallet on the ground.**

   _____

9. **The large dog slobbered all over me.**

   _____

10. **Ellen closed the door after Bob left.**

   _____

The Complete Subject and Predicate

The **complete subject** contains the simple subject and any additional words that tell you who or what the sentence is speaking about. The **complete predicate** contains the simple predicate plus all other words that talk about the actions of the subject or condition of the subject following a linking verb.

Example: The jolly young man / told good jokes all the time.
                     complete subject   complete predicate (with action verb)
                 The jolly young man / is a great joke teller.
                     complete subject   complete predicate (with linking verb)

Underline the complete subject in each sentence once. Underline the complete predicate twice.

1. The celebrated writer Mark Twain was actually a man named Samuel L. Clemens.

2. As a young man, Samuel worked on the riverboats that travelled up and down the Mississippi.

3. The name, Mark Twain, was adapted from a riverboat term.

4. Mark Twain means "two fathoms" deep.

5. His admiring readers think that his writing is much deeper than a mere two fathoms.

6. His first major work was published in 1867.

7. It was a humorous sketch called *The Celebrated Jumping Frog of Calaveras County.*

8. Two years later he wrote the critically acclaimed *Innocents Abroad.*

9. His reputation grew around the world.

10. For the next forty years he wrote some of America's most acclaimed literature.

11. This included essays, autobiographies, travel sketches, novels, and short stories.

12. He perfected the use of American Western dialect in his stories.

13. His writings, although sometimes controversial for their treatment of racial issues, remain fresh and alive today.

14. One of his best-loved works, *The Adventures of Huckleberry Finn,* still flames the imaginations of young people everywhere.

Simple Sentences

A **simple sentence** is composed of one independent clause and usually has *one subject and one verb* (ex. A). It is possible for there to be *more than one subject with the same verb* (ex. B). It is also possible for there to be *more than one verb with the same subject* (ex. C). Finally, it is possible for there to be *more than one subject and more than one verb in a simple sentence* (ex. D). If there are two independent clauses (two complete thoughts and two entirely separate subjects and predicates), *the sentence is no longer classified as simple* (ex. E).

Example: **Simple Sentences**
  A) The portrait / hangs above the fireplace.
  B) That boy and that girl / are great athletes. (compound subject)
  C) We / ate and drank to our hearts' content. (compound verb)
  D) Albert and Beth / can come and meet our friends. (compound subject and verb)
  Not a Simple Sentence
  E) Mary drinks coffee, and Michael drinks tea. (two independent clauses)

Identify the type of simple sentence from the four types listed above. Write A, B, C, or D in the blank. If the sentence is not simple, write E in the blank.

_____ 1. Fourteen girls are invited to the slumber party.

_____ 2. The girl is a gymnast, and her brother is an artist.

_____ 3. The vase and the champagne glasses are fine crystal.

_____ 4. My mom took one look at the mess and shook her head.

_____ 5. She broke her leg and sprained her wrist in the accident.

_____ 6. My teacher and my brother really helped me with the math assignment.

_____ 7. I tossed and turned all night.

_____ 8. Beth is an eighth grader, and Anne is a seventh grader.

_____ 9. *Rigoletto* and *Madame Butterfly* are Patricia's favorite operas.

_____ 10. The woman with the black hair turned and stared at me.

_____ 11. The keyboard and the printer need to be replaced.

_____ 12. Myrtis and Desmond will try to come.

_____ 13. The buffet and the dining room table are being refinished.

_____ 14. She saw the note and couldn't believe her eyes.

_____ 15. I brought cake, and Natalie supplied the punch.

Compound Sentences

A **compound sentence** is two or more simple sentences joined. A sentence with two (or more) subjects, each with its own verb, cannot be simple because it contains more than one complete thought (one clause is not dependent on the other). Most compound sentences are joined by the conjunction *and*, *but*, or *or*. A comma usually comes before the conjunction, unless the two clauses are very short. Occasionally a semicolon (;) can take the place of the conjunction.

Example: The bread was dry, but the cheese was tasty.
            She laughed and he cried.
            I can go; you can't go.

Underline each independent clause in the compound sentences below. Circle the conjunction and/or punctuation that separates the two clauses.

1. I would love your approval, but I don't expect it.

2. Gary finished his essay, and he submitted it on time.

3. The dictionary page tore, and she taped it back together.

4. I will buy some sensible shoes, then I will start jogging daily.

5. He wanted a snack, but the contents of the refrigerator were not inviting.

6. You have your way; I'll have mine.

7. Mother fretted and father fumed.

8. The toast burned and the pancakes stuck.

9. She has a great voice, and she loves to sing opera.

10. Did you break the window or did Brandon do it?

11. Kate cooked the scrumptious feast, and Alex cleaned the house.

12. I haven't decided, but it's time to act.

13. For his birthday we will buy Andrew a tackle box, or we'll take him to the beach.

14. You get the bucket; I'll get the mop.

15. Jim wants to leave but Kelly isn't ready.

Compound Sentences

Read the simple sentences then change each into a compound sentence.

1. **She followed her dream.** _____

_____

_____

2. **Robert loves to ski.** _____

_____

_____

3. **Cheryl is a math whiz.** _____

_____

_____

4. **The clock was wrong.** _____

_____

_____

5. **The child molded an elephant out of clay.** _____

_____

_____

6. **The house looked deserted.** _____

_____

_____

7. **The milk tasted sour.** _____

_____

_____

8. **The glass goblet shattered.** _____

_____

_____

9. **Teresa and Marius attended the matinee.** _____

_____

_____

10. **Perry bought the flowers and sent them.** _____

_____

_____

Simple and Compound Sentences

Write S if the sentence is simple, and C if the sentence is compound.

_____ 1. We followed him into the cemetery, but he seemed to disappear.

_____ 2. The girl in this ad makes a lot of money modeling.

_____ 3. Sherry and Rene love swimming and hiking.

_____ 4. Run and hide.

_____ 5. She petted the dog and teased the cat.

_____ 6. The answer is quite simple, but you still can't figure it out.

_____ 7. White water rafting is fun, but it can be very dangerous.

_____ 8. *Oliver Twist* and *Great Expectations* are her favorite novels by Dickens.

_____ 9. *Macbeth* is a tragic play by Shakespeare, and *Midsummer Night's Dream* is a comedy.

_____ 10. In the pantry we found only a can of peas and a sack of flour.

_____ 11. You can help, or you can leave.

_____ 12. Connie enjoyed the book and will write a favorable book report.

_____ 13. It may be cold, but at least it's not humid.

_____ 14. The quarterback played in the Super Bowl, and then he went to Disney World.

_____ 15. French is his favorite language, and Italian is his favorite type of food.

_____ 16. The lights are lit, but no one appears to be home.

_____ 17. Paul quit his job, but he was not out of work for long.

_____ 18. Walk; don't run.

_____ 19. Hong Kong is an exciting city, but Buenos Aires is my favorite.

_____ 20. The books and the paper must be moved before morning.

Independent and Dependent Clauses

An **independent (main) clause** can stand alone as a sentence. A **dependent (subordinate) clause** contains a subject and verb, but it does not express a complete thought and can't stand alone as a sentence. The dependent clause must be attached to the independent clause to complete the meaning. Dependent clauses often begin with a subordinating conjunction such as *although*, *because*, *if*, *since*, *until*, and *when*. They may also begin with relative pronouns such as *who*, *which*, or *that*.

Example: **Separately:**
Michael bought the painting at an auction. (independent)
which was a Van Gogh (dependent)
After participating in a bidding war (dependent)
Combined to make a sentence:
After participating in a bidding war, Michael bought the painting, which was a Van Gogh, at an auction.
(combination of two dependent and one independent clause)

Identify each clause as independent (IN) or dependent (D). Underline the subordinating conjunction or relative pronoun if there is one. No punctuation or capitalization is provided.

_____ 1. until you understand

_____ 2. since I have cleaned my room

_____ 3. she finished her homework

_____ 4. before he became an archaeologist

_____ 5. We saw an elephant

_____ 6. who buy their tickets in advance

_____ 7. Jean makes the best candy

_____ 8. after the music stopped

_____ 9. the microwave is broken

_____10. which is broken again

_____11. Beth wears sensible walking shoes

_____12. since the walk is long

69

Independent and Dependent Clauses

Identify each clause as independent (IN) or dependent (D). Underline the subordinating conjunction or relative pronoun if there is one. No punctuation or capitalization is provided.

_____ 1. she wears too much makeup

_____ 2. since she is under a lot of stress

_____ 3. until the entire project is complete

_____ 4. we were thirty minutes late for the appointment

_____ 5. because you're afraid

_____ 6. they felt more comfortable with me

_____ 7. if the turkey is not refrigerated

_____ 8. although the report was in plan view

_____ 9. which is in demand

_____10. that I know

_____11. shadows are longer in the winter

_____12. it is homemade

_____13. when the plant is over watered

_____14. it was raining

_____15. because good records were not kept

_____16. until the light bulb was invented

_____17. that I wear to church

_____18. Sal is arachnophobic

_____19. before it can be eaten

_____20. you are strange

70

Dependent Clauses and Other Fragments

A sentence is a complete thought containing a subject and verb. A **dependent clause** is an incomplete thought that has a subject and verb. Other kinds of incomplete sentences are called **fragments**.

Example: She told me. (sentence)
            while I wait (dependent clause)
            running through the crowd (fragment)

Define each group of words as a sentence (S), dependent clause (D), or fragment (F). No punctuation or capitalization is provided.

——— 1. listen to me

——— 2. to listen to them

——— 3. when I listen to them

——— 4. Matt sat next to me

——— 5. who sat next to me

——— 6. next to me

——— 7. when stating his opinion

——— 8. when he stated his opinion

——— 9. he stated his opinion

——— 10. I protested the new rule

——— 11. until I protested

——— 12. protesting the new rule

——— 13. please repeat the question

——— 14. repeating the question

——— 15. who repeated the question

——— 16. Meg defined the word

——— 17. to define the word

——— 18. which defines the word

——— 19. before you go

——— 20. you go

——— 21. before going

——— 22. who lives in a castle

——— 23. like living in a castle

——— 24. who lives in a castle

——— 25. try to win

——— 26. trying to win

——— 27. unless you try to win

——— 28. streaking through the sky

——— 29. it streaked through the sky

——— 30. while it was streaking

——— 31. the alarm rang

——— 32. hearing the alarm

Making Fragments into Sentences

Rewrite each fragment below, making it into a complete sentence.

1. **by reserving a ticket** _____

   _____

2. **watching an old sitcom on television** _____

   _____

3. **to live in the country** _____

   _____

4. **twirling ballerinas on the dance floor** _____

   _____

5. **for conserving energy** _____

   _____

6. **having lost his way** _____

   _____

7. **through the garden and across the pond** _____

   _____

8. **to escape from the wicked warlock** _____

   _____

9. **from the looks of those shoes** _____

   _____

10. **squeezing through a crack in the fence** _____

   _____

Complex Sentences

A **complex sentence** contains one independent clause and one or more dependent clauses. The independent clause is the more important of the two, and the dependent clause modifies it in some way. A dependent clause can appear inside the independent clause as well as before it or after it. It is usually introduced by a subordinating conjunction or a relative pronoun.

Example: When we heard how much the repairs would cost, we decided to buy a new car. We didn't think that we could afford a new car, until we saw the cost of repairs. The girl who is driving the red convertible is my sister.

Write CX if the sentence is complex. Underline the independent clause once. Underline the dependent clause(s) twice.

_____ 1. If you plan the party, I will come.

_____ 2. I will take the early flight if absolutely necessary.

_____ 3. Because of her great personality, Lauren is very popular.

_____ 4. Mr. West, a computer programmer, will help us set up our new computer.

_____ 5. The new teacher who is being evaluated is in Room 306.

_____ 6. When the summer gets hot, Alice longs for snowy mountains.

_____ 7. Since the party is on a school night, I can't go.

_____ 8. The dog that looks like a stray belongs to my neighbor.

_____ 9. The state which is my favorite is Maine.

_____10. Rebecca is my friend who loves animals.

_____11. You must put on your seatbelt before I start the car.

_____12. Whenever we want great homemade pie, we go to my grandmother's house.

_____13. Because you are my friend, I will tell you my secret!

_____14. The girl wearing the yellow headband is my sister.

_____15. Mrs. Scott, who was my third grade teacher, is my new neighbor.

Complex Sentences

Underline the dependent clause in each complex sentence. Do nothing to the sentence if it is not complex.

1. My sister, who spends most of her time at the library, is an avid reader of nonfiction in the area of environmental concerns.

2. Until you clean your room and wash the dog, don't expect to get your weekly allowance.

3. The Mexican tour operator in Cancun specializes in tours that introduce foreign visitors to local Mayan Indians.

4. Alex is a friendly and energetic person who loves to be in the middle of active group projects.

5. If each class contributes a Thanksgiving basket with all the trimmings, our school will be able to help forty needy families.

6. The science fiction writer Isaac Asimov is able to create a whole new world that is completely foreign to us.

7. In Malaysia we saw a temple with a reclining Buddha and big dragons out front which made for a good photo opportunity.

8. Since I didn't give the elephant the bananas fast enough, she gave me a special spray of water with her trunk.

9. It is easy to catch a taxi in New York, although the drivers often don't speak much English.

10. If you enjoy visiting old southern plantations, try Nottaway Plantation in Donaldsonville, Louisiana.

11. Alice Walker, who is best known for her novels, has also written several books of poetry.

12. Ralph, who is rarely at home, has an active social life.

13. Although the necklace was very inexpensive, Cheryl cherished it for sentimental reasons.

14. Until night fell, my whole family worked tirelessly in our newly-planted vegetable garden.

15. By the time she was twenty, Kendall had finished her bachelor's degree in Anthropology.

Complex Sentence Review

Classify each of the following sentences as follows:

(**S**)Simple   (**C**)Compound   (**CX**)Complex.

_____ 1. If you need any help, I'm available.

_____ 2. You won't believe what I found out.

_____ 3. Mrs. Meyers wants to go to New Zealand, but her husband would prefer to go to Kenya.

_____ 4. Peggy isn't paying attention in class today.

_____ 5. Clarissa and I have been best friends since fifth grade, and we probably always will be best friends.

_____ 6. I think that the artist who does the best portraits is this one.

_____ 7. We spent two hours on the tour bus, and then we began a walking tour of London.

_____ 8. Betty would be a good writer if she would only be more conscientious about revising.

_____ 9. I actually witnessed the shoplifter take an expensive watch and slip it in his pocket.

_____10. I know him because we went to the same summer camp last year.

_____11. I was confused about the time until I noticed that the electricity had gone out.

_____12. I want you to come, but it is your decision.

_____13. Drew's birthday is on Thursday, and I can't think of a really good present for him.

_____14. Meghan has a schedule conflict this weekend that she doesn't know how to resolve.

_____15. Patricia looked stunning in the blue suit.

_____16. Sam has several inventions patented, and he is hard at work on another one.

_____17. Alyssa has been enjoying books from a very early age.

_____18. My cat awakens me a dawn every morning.

_____19. After he gets a good bath, my dog can't wait to roll in the dirt.

_____20. Will you be responsible for collecting the money?

Complex Sentence Review

Classify each of the following sentences as follows:
(**S**)Simple   (**C**)Compound   (**CX**)Complex

_____ 1. Father put the baby to bed at seven o'clock, but she didn't fall asleep for a long time.

_____ 2. William Shakespeare wrote plays and poetry.

_____ 3. After I finish practicing piano, I'll help you make the fudge.

_____ 4. We heard the siren and saw the police car.

_____ 5. Meghan couldn't wake up this morning.

_____ 6. When Germaine saw Keisha, it was love at first sight.

_____ 7. Carla would prefer to vacation in the Caribbean, but I'd rather spend time in Europe.

_____ 8. Many of Jane Austen's novels have been made into successful movies over the past forty years.

_____ 9. Because she couldn't swim a stroke, Vicki didn't enjoy boating or any water-related recreation.

_____ 10. The flimsy cover of the dictionary fell off from constant use.

_____ 11. I need to shorten the hem of this dress and add new buttons if I'm going to wear it for another season.

_____ 12. Beth takes French and Bob takes Spanish.

_____ 13. A live performance of _The Nutcracker_ or _Swan Lake_ is always a treat for ballet lovers.

_____ 14. Carl felt much better when his diet improved.

_____ 15. After we decorated the Christmas tree, we stood back and admired our work.

_____ 16. The school play is this weekend, but I won't be able to attend.

_____ 17. Our sofa converts into a double bed.

_____ 18. Are you fond of winter, or do you prefer the summer?

_____ 19. When Jasmine can't sleep, she drinks warm milk.

_____ 20. Are you just arriving or just leaving?

Complex Sentence Review

Classify each of the following sentences as follows:
(S) Simple   **(C)**Compound   **(CX)**Complex

(1) The islands of Hawaii are a world of their own. (2) Each has a distinct flavor, yet all share in the heavenly beauty of the tropics. (3) The most likely spot to begin exploring is Honolulu, Oahu which is the island with famous Waikiki Beach. (4) One special sight here is the natural puka in the rugged coastline known as the Blow Hole. (5) A geyser effect is created by the action of the waves being forced through the lava tube. (6) Also to be found in Oahu is the Iolani Palace, the only house of royalty on American soil. (7) Finally, on this island few visitors miss the opportunity to see USS Arizona Battleship Memorial in Pearl Harbor.

(8) Maui, the second largest island, is considered by many to be the most beautiful. (9) It contains the world's largest dormant volcano, and it is known for its spectacular sunsets and great beaches. (10) Another famous sight to view is the Iao Needle, a 1,200-foot green monolith, which rises hauntingly from the valley floor. (11) The old whaling seaport of Lahaina with its quaint streets and shops is another Maui treasure. (12) From the eastern shore at Hana, the ocean stretches seemingly forever, and it is alive with coral and exotically colored fish.

(13) The Big Island, Hawaii, is the youngest and southernmost in the chain. (14) It contains Volcanoes National Park which was established to preserve the mysteriously beautiful landscape of Mauna Loa volcano and its active neighbor Kilaueau. (15) Kilaueau erupts regularly and in spectacular style with steaming fire pits and giant lava tubes. (16) A popular activity is flightseeing over the volcanoes from a helicopter.

(17) Another unique island is Kauai with its famous Fern Grotto which is a secluded cave framed by gigantic fishtail ferns. (18) A not-to-be-missed sight is the Waimea Canyon, often called the "Grand Canyon of the Pacific." (19) Here you will see green jungles, and breathtaking waterfalls, cliffs and canyons. (20) Hawaii has something for everyone, and, therefore, it is one of the world's favorite destinations for tourists.

1. _____	6. _____	11. _____	16. _____
2. _____	7. _____	12. _____	17. _____
3. _____	8. _____	13. _____	18. _____
4. _____	9. _____	14. _____	19. _____
5. _____	10. _____	15. _____	20. _____

Sentence Expanding with When, Where, and How

Read the core sentence. Expand it to include information about *when*, *where*, or *how* it happened.

Example: Chad worked on his research project.
                    tirelessly   (how)
                    at the library   (where)
                    everyday after school   (when)
            Chad worked tirelessly on his research project at the library
            everyday after school.

1. **Mario found the path.**

_____

_____

2. **The rain poured.**

_____

_____

3. **We descended the mountain trail.**

_____

_____

4. **Beth concocted an original dessert.**

_____

_____

5. **Evelyn planned her spring garden.**

_____

_____

6. **Senator Blair continued campaigning.**

_____

_____

Sentence Combining

Read the two sentences. Underline the part in the second sentence which can be used to expand the first sentence. Rewrite the first sentence to include the underlined information. No changes in words or punctuation are necessary.

Example: The children should not see that film.
The children are <u>below thirteen years of age</u>.
The children below thirteen years of age should not see that film.

1. **The candidates will speak at the university.**
The candidates are running for governor.

   _____

   _____

2. **The road construction is to be completed by next June.**
The road construction is causing heavy traffic at this time.

   _____

   _____

3. **These students are taking advanced placement courses.**
These students are in their senior year.

   _____

   _____

4. **The fund raiser should produce considerable revenue.**
The fund raiser is scheduled for next month.

   _____

   _____

5. **The neighborhood filed a grievance.**
The neighborhood is receiving assistance from the Environmental Protection Agency.

   _____

   _____

Pronouns after *Than* and *As*

When a sentence compares one person to another using **than** or **as**, the pronoun used after than or as may be either in the nominative case (*I, you, he, she, we, they*) or the objective case (*me, you, him, her,* or *them*). To determine which case is correct, expand the sentence.

Example: Mike is shorter than I. (nominative case needed)
Mike is shorter than I am.
Jane is not as talented as she. (nominative case needed)
Jane is not as talented as she is.
Cliff likes Alice more than me. (objective case needed)
Cliff likes Alice better than he likes me.
Brad likes Alice more than I. (nominative case needed)
Brad likes Alice more than I like Alice.

Circle the pronoun in the correct case. Write the expanded sentence. If there are two possible expanded sentences, circle both pronouns and write both expanded sentences.

1. **Luciano sings as well as (I, me).**

_____

_____

2. **Manuel is not as well known as (he, him).**

_____

_____

3. **Gigi knows him better than (I, me).**

_____

_____

4. **Roger delivered a better speech than (she, her).**

_____

_____

5. **Jeff loves Becky more than (I, me).**

_____

_____

6. **Jack can run faster than (he, him).**

_____

_____

Who, Whom, Whoever, and Whomever

Who and **whoever** are used as subjects of verbs (nominatives). **Whom** and **whomever** are used as direct objects (objects of verbs) or objects of prepositions.

Example: Jack is the one <u>who</u> got caught. (*who* is the subject of *got*)
<u>Whoever</u> owns this credit card must first show identification.
   (*whoever* is the subject of the verb *owns*)
Give this to <u>whomever</u> you want. (*whomever* is object of the preposition *to*)
That is the woman whom I saw on the train.
   (*whom* is direct object of the verb *saw*)

Fill in the blank with the correct pronoun—*who, whoever, whom*, or *whomever*.

1. Jack asked Jill _____ she invited to the dance.

2. With everyone in costume, I don't know _____ is who.

3. Vote for _____ you want.

4. This is a lady _____ is worthy of your trust.

5. I know _____ it was that cheated.

6. Miss Scarlet is the guest _____ committed murder.

7. _____ is responsible for this mess?

8. Mr. Washington is the man _____ we met.

9. Can you guess _____ we saw at the mall?

10. The mysterious woman _____ was here left you a message.

11. Please ask _____ is nearby to come and help.

12. The person to _____ I gave the money has vanished.

Who's & Whose

Who's is a contraction for *Who is*. **Whose** can be an interrogative pronoun that indicates pos-session or a relative pronoun (introducing a clause) in the possessive case.

Example: Who's coming? (contraction for *Who is*)
Whose recipe is this? (interrogative pronoun showing possession)
The man whose recipe won first place is from Louisiana.
(relative pronoun showing possession)

Fill in the blank with *who's* or *whose*. Decide how the word is used and label it as a contraction (C), interrogative (INT), or relative pronoun (RP).

_____ 1. _____ name did you pick?

_____ 2. _____ your first choice for class president?

_____ 3. I know _____ name you picked.

_____ 4. _____ going to pick up the children after school?

_____ 5. _____ mother is carpooling today?

_____ 6. That is the girl _____ mother is driving today.

_____ 7. _____ signature is this?

_____ 8. _____ the most likely one to get caught?

_____ 9. The student _____ report card had all A's was the
envy of everyone.

_____ 10. _____ ten dollar bill is this on the ground?

_____ 11. _____ the owner of this ten dollar bill?

_____ 12. The woman _____ picture hangs in the office is a
former principal.

Their, There and *They're*

Their is a pronominal adjective that is the possessive form of *they*. **There** is an adverb meaning "at that place or at that point." **They're** is a pronoun and verb contracted from *they are.*

Example: Do you know <u>their</u> address? (the address belongs to them)
<u>There</u> is the bibliography. (at that place)
<u>They're</u> merely acquaintances. (contraction of *they are*)

Write either *their, there* or *they're* in the blanks below.

1. _____ won't be time for a thorough review of the material.

2. I don't want to ruin _____ plans.

3. Do you know _____ motivation?

4. _____ the likely culprits.

5. _____ tickets to Singapore are first class.

6. I can't find _____ address.

7. _____ is a detour due to construction just up the road.

8. _____ wasn't anything worth watching on television.

9. _____ not to be trusted.

10. _____ first choice of vacation spots was Maui.

11. _____ will be a fifteen minute break at four o'clock.

12. Did you see _____ reaction?

Write one sentence for each of the words *their, there*, and *they're.*

13. (their) _____

14. (there) _____

15. (they're) _____

Your and *You're*

Your is the possessive form of *you.* **You're** is the contraction for *you are.*

    Example: I know <u>your</u> secret. (the secret belongs to you)
                   <u>You're</u> the people's choice. (contraction of *you are*)

Correctly fill in the blank with *your* or *you're.*

1. I don't know _____ name.

2. _____ the cause of all this.

3. I am impressed with _____ proposal.

4. I don't like what _____ thinking.

5. _____ suggestion is a good one.

6. _____ not serious!

7. _____ the most likely applicant to get the position.

8. I think that these are _____ earrings.

9. Is that _____ dog?

10. _____ the only one left.

11. What is _____ social security number?

12. Is _____ decision made?

13. _____ perfect for the part.

14. What is _____ opinion?

15. _____ welcome to come.

16. I found _____ sweater in my closet.

Its and *It's*

It's is a contraction for *it is* or *it has*. **Its** is the possessive form of *it*.

Example: It's the wrong phone number. (contraction of *it is*)
The neighborhood lost its electrical power. (power belongs to it)

Correctly fill in each blank with *it's* or *its*.

1. _____ time to make a decision.

2. The navy squadron must follow _____ orders.

3. Do you know _____ brand name?

4. _____ the wrong path.

5. Virtue is _____ own reward.

6. Do you know if _____ time to go?

7. _____ odor is unmistakable.

8. _____ value has not yet been determined.

9. No one is sure of _____ origin.

10. _____ still broken.

11. Everything was in _____ place.

12. _____ cause was unclear.

13. _____ my sister's bicycle.

14. _____ not your concern.

15. If _____ raining, we'll call off the hike.

Than and *Then*

Then is an adverb of time. **Than** is a conjunction used in clauses of comparison.

Example: She <u>then</u> finished her homework. (tells when she finished)
             She felt better today <u>than</u> yesterday . (compares *today* and *yesterday*)

Fill in each blank using *then* or *than* correctly.

1. **The watch costs more now _____ it did two weeks ago.**

2. **He thought that he could handle the money better _____ I could.**

3. **And _____ there were none.**

4. **You go first, _____ I'll go.**

5. **You pick it out, _____ I'll buy it.**

6. **I'd rather go tonight _____ this afternoon.**

7. **The cat would rather be snoozing _____ playing.**

8. **Bob enjoys basketball more _____ fishing.**

9. **Marinate the steak and _____ put it in the refrigerator overnight.**

10. **Hubert plays piano better _____ Jeremy.**

11. **Turn on the computer, _____ open the file.**

12. **If you go, _____ I'll go too.**

13. **_____ it will be Mark's turn.**

14. **Do you know what happened _____?**

15. **I like the fir tree more _____ the spruce tree.**

Double Negatives

One negative word makes an entire sentence negative. Using a second negative word
(**double negative**) in the same sentence is not acceptable. *Barely, scarcely, never,* and *hardly*
are considered negatives, as well as *not, no, no one,* and *nothing.*

Example: I <u>scarcely</u> got <u>no</u> sleep last night. (double negative is incorrect)
              I <u>scarcely</u> got <u>any</u> sleep last night. (correct)

Rewrite each sentence so that there is not a double negative.

1. I couldn't hardly wait for summer camp.

   _____

   _____

2. Valerie never had no acceptable excuses for her frequent tardiness.

   _____

   _____

3. Clarice didn't never see him again.

   _____

   _____

4. My parents said that there wasn't no way that I could go.

   _____

   _____

5. Nothing never thrilled me more than my first sight of Notre Dame Cathedral in Paris.

   _____

   _____

6. No one had nothing to say about the incident.

   _____

   _____

7. I hadn't never realized how destructive gossip could be.

   _____

   _____

8. I don't like to play no card games.

   _____

   _____

Capitalization of Titles

Capitalize the title of books, movies, poems, songs, television programs, and works of art. Do not capitalize words such as *the, and, on, by,* and *of* unless they are the first word in the title.

Rewrite the titles in the sentences that follow using capitals correctly.

1. (*mutiny on the bounty*) _____ , written by

   Nordhoff and Hal, is possibly the greatest sea story of all time.

2. (*the hobbit*) _____ is a fantasy written by

   J.R. Tolkien which is enjoyed by children and adults alike.

3. (*sunset boulevard*) _____ , the musical

   sensation, was written by Andrew Lloyd Webber.

4. (*lord of the flies*) In 1954 William Golding wrote a book entitled _____

   _____ about a group of English school boys stranded without

   adults on a desert island.

5. (*paradise lost*) John Milton wrote an epic poem called _____

   about the creation of the world.

6. (*the cosby show*)   One of the most popular family sitcoms of all time was

   _____ .

7. (*stopping by the woods on a snowy evening*) One of the most musical and haunting

   poems written by Robert Frost is _____ .

8. (*roll of thunder, hear my cry*) Mildred Taylor, who won the 1977 Newbery Medal for her

   realistic portrayal of black family life in rural Mississippi in the early 1930s, dedicated

   the book _____ to the memory of her

   father.

Name _____   **Capitalization**

Word Capitalization

Use an initial capital letter to mark proper nouns (Ben Franklin), or adjectives (Chinese), titles of distinction (Prince of Wales), races, religions, and ethnic groups (Caucasian, Buddhist), official bodies (the United States Senate), and geographic divisions (the East Side).

Underline the word(s) that should be capitalized.

1. hans holzer, a famous psychic investigator, has written a number of books on ghosts and writes on this topic regularly for national magazines, motion pictures, and television.
2. He has investigated haunted places in europe from scotland to austria and has many tales to tell.
3. One of the most celebrated haunted places is the tower of london.
4. anne boleyn, the second wife of henry viii who was beheaded for supposed infidelity, has been seen walking headless in the salt tower in the tower of london.
5. longleat in somerset is one of the most publicized haunted houses in england.
6. It seems that at least four ghosts haunt this stately dwelling: the lady louisa, who mourned the violent death of her lover, the slaughtered rebel from the duke of mon mouth's army, the builder of longleat, sir john thynne, and the wealthy owner, thomas thynne, who was murdered by a certain lieutenant stern.
7. In scotland is a small house by the name of croft-en-reigh which stands in back of holyrood palace, once the residence of mary queen of scots.
8. Her ghost, who had often been to this house in times of great emotional turmoil, has supposedly been seen here, as well as the sixteenth century french architect who built the place.
9. Another european haunted house is ross house in ireland, which stands on a bluff looking directly into clew bay, halfway between westport and newport.
10. One ghost is that of a maid in a starched blue and white uniform named annie o'flynn, who was a very loyal servant to one of the former families.
11. Another former owner who has been frequently observed in the garden and on the stairs at ross house is the sea captain, who died at sea, but has been observed by many, always in the daylight, and always smoking a cigar.
12. One haunted site in france, built during the second empire in the 1860s by emperor napoleon iii, is located in the suburbs of paris.
13. napoleon kept a lonely mistress there, and she played her grand piano constantly.
14. Until the house was finally abandoned, numerous people who slept there in the parisian suburb of maison-lafitte heard loud nocturnal music from their bedrooms above the salon that contained the grand piano.

Commas to Separate Dates and Addresses

Use commas to separate parts of dates and addresses. Do not separate the ZIP code from the city and state with a comma.

Example: The battle of New Orleans was fought on March 13, 1815.
The New York Convention and Visitor's Bureau is located at:
2 Columbus Circle, New York, New York 10019.
We left on Monday, July 5th.

Add commas to correctly complete the following sentences.

1. The package was sent on November 11 1994, but did not arrive until January 4 1996.

2. Mr. Harper's retirement will begin on Monday April 11 1997.

3. The Duponts will stay at a hotel at 40 Avenue Victor Hugo Aix-en-Provence France.

4. If you think nothing of spending $500.00 for a pair of shoes, go to Via Veneto 98 Rome Italy to shop.

5. Her pen pal's address is 4700 Main Street Kansas City Kansas 22980.

6. The first performance of Giuseppe Verdi's Rigoletto was at La Fenice Theatre in Venice on March 11 1851.

7. The address on the postcard was 81 Mariani Avenue Cupertino California 95014-6299.

8. Which catalog company is located at 1 Lands' End Dodgeville Wisconsin 53539?

9. The baby was born on April 19 1995 in Mobile Alabama.

10. My new job begins in September in Grand Rapids Michigan.

11. The September 14 1991 issue of *Time* has an article on the presidential candidates.

12. On Saturday July 17 1995 my sister married her high school sweetheart.

13. The deposit for the senior class trip is due no later than Friday February 3 1995.

14. Please send all entries to 501 Post Street San Francisco California 94102.

15. I will always remember Christmas 1972.

16. Send your resume to P.O. Box 89710 Dallas Texas 75202.

17. My dentist appointment is set for 3 o'clock on Monday March 15.

18. Many Gulf Coast resorts are located on Sandestin Boulevard South in Destin Florida.

Commas to Separate Independent Clauses

Use a comma to separate independent clauses joined by the coordinating conjunctions: *and, but, yet, nor,* or *yet* unless each clause is very short.

Example: Brad will bring a variety of snacks, and Sarah will bring three or four videos.
The sky darkened and the rain fell. (two short independent clauses)
The sky darkened and sounded menacing. (only one independent clause)

Place commas where appropriate in each sentence. Leave the sentence blank if no punctuation is needed.

1. The time was midnight and my homework still wasn't finished.

2. She agrees and he disagrees.

3. I did not know her name but she looked very familiar.

4. Whales are mammals and they must come to the surface of the water for air.

5. We waited in front of the school but our ride did not come.

6. Frank heard the news and he quickly told his friends.

7. Celeste looked everywhere but her bracelet was gone.

8. We could go Christmas shopping today or we could wait until the weekend.

9. Are you planning to attend college in town or will you be looking elsewhere?

10. The hotel room had a beautiful view but it was too small.

11. We were exhausted yet we couldn't get to sleep.

12. That test should be very difficult or I shall be surprised.

13. Parking downtown is a nuisance and it is very expensive.

14. Sean is a good writer but he is a lousy typist.

15. The choice seems obvious yet I can't decide.

16. The Jacksons love skiing and they go every winter.

17. I went skiing once but I wasn't very good at it.

18. Will you be coming with my sister or driving yourself?

19. Carl likes fishing but Victor prefers mountain climbing.

20. Our home is rather small but we don't mind.

Commas to Separate Dependent from Independent Clauses

Use a comma to separate a dependent (subordinate) clause from the main clause when the subordinate clause comes first.

Example: Before Kern began her recipe, she made sure she had all the ingredients.

Place commas where appropriate.

1. Although I like snow skiing exploring the ruins of a Gothic castle is my favorite.

2. While Crystal swam many laps Bob sunbathed.

3. Because they cater to teens these shops are not too expensive.

4. When I finally passed the big sign welcoming me to Window Rock Arizona I noticed that I was out of gas.

5. Since she loves rugged sports Norma would like to try paragliding.

6. If you enjoy German cooking try sauerbraten.

7. While we relaxed on our hotel balcony we enjoyed a panoramic vista of Santa Fe and spectacular views of the Sangre de Cristo Mountains.

8. After we visited a museum we had lunch at a sunny outdoor cafe.

9. Because they see divers so constantly the green sea turtles which live in the Sheraton Caverns in Kauai, Hawaii are not afraid of people.

10. While most wild animals prefer flight to fight you must consider that they can be dangerous and unpredictable.

11. As the terrain opened up below me I nearly fell off my chair in the ski lift.

12. Since I love to write my Brazilian pen pal and I exchanged countless letters.

13. If you enjoy snowmobile races try the Iron Dog Race between Wasilla and Nome, Alaska.

14. Until Snowshoe Thompson took the job of mailman-on-skis in 1856 in the Sierra Nevada there had been virtually no communication between the remote mining towns and the rest of the world in the winter.

15. If you hate cold feet it is possible to buy a compact, battery-operated foot warming system.

Commas with Introductory Prepositional Phrase

Use a comma following two or more introductory prepositional phrases.

Example: In the afternoon after lunch, we visited the museum.

Insert a comma where needed. Leave the sentence blank if it is already correct.

1. In spite of the warning about the bad weather Albert went boating anyway.

2. Tomorrow afternoon we will pick up Jack and his family at the airport.

3. With the money in her hand she bought the expensive car with the convertible top.

4. After the beginning of the parade we decided that it was too crowded and left.

5. In the darkness in front of the car I saw a wild animal quickly dart across the road.

6. At dinner Patty told us the good news and made us promise to keep it a secret.

7. Around the corner there is a gourmet grocery store.

8. On the freshly mopped floor a long trail of fresh dog prints could be seen.

9. With the increase in price we decided to settle for a less expensive model.

10. After the long, hot summer we were happy to welcome the brisk fall weather.

11. In spite of my vehement protests the policeman gave me a speeding ticket.

12. The girl the in the picture wearing the lavender velvet dress is my youngest sister.

13. Across the table sat a man with a sour expression on his bearded face.

14. Between Birch and Pine Street is a neighborhood grocery store, dry cleaners, and drug store.

15. After June of this year Ms. Jackson will be able to retire from teaching.

Commas with Interrupters

Commas are used to set apart expressions that interrupt a sentence. These include: appositives and appositive phrases, words used in direct address, and parenthetical expressions or other interrupters that are not essential to the meaning of the sentence (such as *however, on the other hand, obviously, in my opinion, of course,* or *therefore*).

      Example: We saw Bill, the new kid, standing by his locker. (appositive phrase)
                       Paul, I hold you responsible for this. (direct address)
                       This pie, in my opinion, should win the blue ribbon. (parenthetical expressions)

Place commas where needed. In the blank, tell if the comma separates an appositive or appositive phrase (A), a direct address (D), or parenthetical expressions (P).

_____ 1. The answer of course is twenty-one.

_____ 2. Sarah the tallest girl is a great volleyball player.

_____ 3. I told you Brandon to leave me alone.

_____ 4. *Sunset Boulevard* Andrew Lloyd Webber's latest musical is playing to packed houses in New York and London.

_____ 5. The murderer my dear Watson must be a woman.

_____ 6. Le Petit Theatre du Vieux Carre the oldest theatre in the south is located in New Orleans.

_____ 7. Fido stop that barking!

_____ 8. Jessica Lange in my opinion should have won the Oscar.

_____ 9. Barry call your sister to the phone.

_____10. I told you Ann to stop putting it off.

_____11. George Bailey a man with high ideals is a beloved character from a movie called *It's a Wonderful Life*.

_____12. Mrs. Clark the hardest seventh grade English teacher gave me an A on my essay.

Quotation Marks

Quotation marks enclose the words used by a speaker or writer. Periods and commas go inside the closing quotation mark in the preferred American style. A comma is used to set off a direct quote from the rest of the sentence. Question marks and exclamation points go inside the closing quotation marks only when they apply to the quoted words. Indirect quotations do not use quotation marks.

Example: "Come here," said Marie. (comma inside)
Marie said, "Come here." (comma used to set off direct quote, period inside)
"Won't you come?" asked Marie. (question mark inside)
Did you hear Marie ask, "Won't you come"? (question mark outside)
Marie asked that I come. (indirect quotation)

Rewrite each sentence using quotation marks, punctuation, and capitalization where needed. Do not change indirect quotations.

1. What happened to you asked Melissa.

_____

_____

2. I slipped and sprained my ankle responded Nina.

_____

_____

3. Melissa asked how she had sprained her ankle.

_____

_____

4. Nina confessed it was my new spiked-heel shoes.

_____

_____

5. I warned you about those things chided Melissa.

_____

_____

6. But they look so good on me insisted Nina.

_____

_____

Name _____

Indirect and Direct Quotations

Quotation marks enclose the words used by a speaker or writer. Periods and commas go inside the closing quotation mark in the preferred American style. A comma is used to set off a direct quote from the rest of the sentence. Question marks and exclamation points go inside the closing quotation marks only when they apply to the quoted words. Indirect quotations do not use quotation marks.

Example: "I like this book," said Paula. (comma inside)
Paula said, "Come here." (comma used to set off direct quote, period inside)
"What is your name?" asked Stevan. (question mark inside)
Did you hear Carol ask, "What is your name"? (question mark outside)
Debbie asked me to bring this. (indirect quotation)

Rewrite the indirect quotations as direct quotations. Rewrite the direct quotations as indirect quotations.

1. The waiter said that the entree would be out shortly.

_____

_____

2. "Do you know her pediatrician?" asked Mr. Howell.

_____

_____

3. She suddenly asked where I was going.

_____

_____

4. "Can I help you?" asked the saleslady.

_____

_____

5. Maxwell said, " I also need four trays of pansies and some mulch."

_____

_____

6. The teacher requested that everyone bring two number 2 pencils for the exam.

_____

_____

Comma Review

Add commas as needed to the following passage.

Many people dream of seeing lions elephants and cheetahs in the wild but an African Safari takes you into the best game preserves for life-size encounters with these amazing creatures. Kenya and Tanzania two areas in Africa famous for their safari adventures provide good starting points.

Before you embark on your first safari you should prepare yourself by attending a presentation on national park reserves and wildlife given by the East African Wild Life Society. Founded in 1961 the East African Wildlife Society uses the proceeds from membership fees to support research and education to conduct surveys and anti-poaching patrols and to rescue and relocate endangered animals. The presentation will help you to more fully understand and appreciate what lies ahead.

The most common way to travel in a safari is by minibus and there is a roof hatch for stand-up viewing for those who care to get an unobstructed view of the animals. Don't worry. Everyone has a window seat and there are ample photo opportunities.

The Samburu Game Reserve named for the tribe living in the area is a popular area for safaris. One animal that you will undoubtedly see is the seemingly tame olive baboon. Other seldom seen wildlife in this preserve include the thin-striped Gervy's zebra reticulated giraffe blue-necked Somali ostrich and Beisa oryx.

Another spectacular place for viewing is Aberdare National Park. It contains the world-famous lodges Treetops and The Ark known for their salt licks and water holes where wildlife come to drink. You can watch the animals that come from the comfort of your viewing deck for as long as you like.

For a once-in-a-lifetime opportunity make reservations for an early morning hot air balloon ride over the Serengeti Plain. Masai Mara the northern extension of Tanzania's Serengeti is home to vast herds of plains game such as wildebeest zebra antelope and gazelle. This afternoon of game viewing takes you to the animals' favorite haunts including the wooded area riverbanks and vast grassy plains.

If you haven't had your fill go to Olduvai Gorge where Dr. Leakey discovered a skull reputed to be from an early hominid. Here you will see the Ngorongoro Crater an extinct collapsed volcano. The crater's floor is 102 square miles and there is a lake in the center. An all terrain vehicle drive you through the crater floor where lions elephants rhinos leopards water buffaloes hyenas and cheetahs abound.

Capitals, Commas, and Quotation Marks Review

Read the following conversation. Underline any word that needs a capital letter. Add commas and quotation marks as needed in each sentence.

1. How would you like to go with me on a four day cruise of the galapagos Islands? Max casually remarked to matthew.

2. Sure why not? responded Matthew.

3. By the way max what will we be seeing there?

4. How about marine iguana sea lions giant tortoises frigate birds and strange rock formations? suggested Max.

5. Max asked Matthew rather sheepishly Where are the galapagos Islands?

6. Well first we will need to get to Quito Ecuador's capital which rests at an altitude of 9,350 feet in the andes Mountains.

7. The Galapagos Islands are right off shore from Quito I suppose suggested matthew.

8. No not really said Max we still have quite a way to go.

9. Max continued Next we'll take the Expreso Metropolitan train through the Andes Mountains down *devil's Nose* a nearly vertical 1,000 foot cliff.

10. Cool replied Matthew.

11. From there continued Max we will come to the flatlands of the coastal jungle where we'll catch a small plane and we'll fly over the Pacific to baltra Isle.

12. That is where we will board the cruise boat I suppose said Matthew.

13. Right Baltra is in the center of the fifteen island Galapagos archipelago and we'll cruise for four days through these volcanic islands.

14. After going to all that trouble to get there I hope we'll be seeing something really unusual Matthew stated.

15. How about some land iguanas a forest of opuntia cactus and some blue-footed boobies?

16. Okay I've got to admit that you've captured my interest said Matthew "What else will we see?

17. On the beach of Punta suarex I hear that there is something called the waved albatross with a wingspan of eight feet offered Max and there are giant tortoises in the interior of the santa cruz island.

18. Personally I'm most interested in Puerta Egas where we'll be surrounded by marine iguana pelicans sea lions penguins and fur seals continued Max with his endless information.

Answer Pages

Identification of Nouns

A noun names a person, place, or thing. Nouns can name specific or general persons, places, and things. They can also name ideas as well as things which can be perceived through the senses.

Example: <u>Mary</u> is my best <u>friend</u>.
Only <u>boys</u> go to that <u>school</u>.
The <u>subject</u> of the <u>book</u> was <u>democracy</u>.

Underline each noun in the narrative that follows.

The Neutral Ground

A few <u>years</u> before <u>Louisiana</u> became a <u>state</u> in <u>1812,</u> there was a famous boundary <u>dispute</u> between the <u>United States</u> and <u>Spain</u>. During that <u>period</u> the <u>United States</u> had acquired the <u>Louisiana Territory</u>, and <u>Spain</u> was in <u>control</u> of what is now <u>Texas</u>. To settle the boundary <u>dispute</u> a neutral <u>strip</u> was created in <u>1806</u> in an <u>agreement</u> between <u>General James Wilkerson</u> of the <u>United States</u> and the Spanish <u>commander</u> at <u>Los Adaes</u>. The <u>land</u> was located between the <u>Sabine River</u> to the <u>west</u> and the <u>Calcasieu River</u> to the <u>east</u>. It was known as the <u>Neutral Ground</u>, or "<u>No Man's Land</u>."

Neither the <u>laws</u> of the <u>United States</u> nor the <u>laws</u> of <u>Spain</u> applied to this forty-mile-wide <u>region</u>. Therefore, it was a large <u>area</u> of ungoverned <u>territory</u> that attracted all <u>kinds</u> of <u>people</u>. <u>Outlaws</u> of both <u>nations</u> quickly settled in the <u>area</u>. <u>Judges</u> sometimes even sentenced <u>criminals</u> to the <u>Neutral Ground</u>. <u>Holdups</u> were frequent for <u>travelers</u> heading <u>west</u> through the <u>strip</u>. <u>Slaves</u> were attracted to the <u>area</u> with the <u>promise</u> of <u>freedom</u>, but <u>outlaws</u> such as <u>Jean Lafitte</u> the <u>pirate</u> captured and sold them. Some <u>people</u> in the <u>area</u> were actually former <u>outlaws</u> trying to start a new <u>life</u> where the <u>law</u> could not touch them.

It had been warned from the <u>beginning</u> that this <u>territory</u> would be the <u>home</u> of every <u>kind</u> of <u>smuggler</u> and <u>outlaw</u> known to <u>man</u>. This <u>warning</u> proved to be very <u>true</u>. It took a <u>total</u> of fifteen <u>years</u> for the boundary <u>dispute</u> to be settled. The <u>Neutral Ground</u> was finally given to the <u>United States</u> in <u>1819</u>, but the <u>legacy</u> of lawless <u>activity</u> did not instantly disappear just because an <u>agreement</u> was signed.

© Carson-Dellosa CD-3744   1

Common and Proper Nouns

A proper noun names a particular person, place, or thing and must always be capitalized. Nouns that are not proper nouns are common nouns.

Example: (Chip) is my <u>cousin</u> who lives in the <u>state</u> of (Idaho).
proper   common   common   proper

In each sentence circle the proper nouns and underline the common nouns.

1. The (Aegean Sea) is located between (Greece) and (Turkey.)
2. The <u>capital</u> of the state of (Texas) is (Austin.)
3. The mountain <u>range</u> called the (Alps) is not only located in the <u>country</u> of (Switzerland,) but also in (France,) (Germany,) (Austria,) and (Italy.)
4. The largest <u>exhibit</u> of paintings and sketches by (Vincent Van Gogh) is on <u>display</u> in a <u>museum</u> in (Amsterdam.)
5. (Beethoven,) the renowned <u>composer</u>, was born in (Bonn, Germany.)
6. The <u>subject</u> of vampires is widely explored in <u>books</u> and in <u>movies.</u>
7. <u>President</u> (Thomas Jefferson) sent <u>expeditions</u> to explore the <u>territory</u> called the (Louisiana Purchase.)
8. The (Trojan War) is reputed to have started as the result of a beauty <u>contest</u> between the <u>goddesses</u> (Minerva,) (Juno,) and (Venus.)
9. (Times Square) is in the <u>heart</u> of the <u>theatre</u> <u>district</u> in (New York.)
10. The (Arenal Volcano) erupts regularly in (Costa Rica.)
11. A <u>flight</u> on the (Concorde) will take you from (New York) to (Paris) in four <u>hours.</u>
12. The <u>abacus</u> is the oldest calculating <u>machine</u> known to <u>man.</u>
13. The (San Diego Zoo) is one of the most famous in the (United States.)
14. (Mardi Gras,) the (French Quarter,) and great <u>food</u> draw many <u>tourists</u> to (New Orleans.)

© Carson-Dellosa CD-3744   2

Compound Nouns

A compound noun is a combination of two or more words to form a new word that is used as a single noun. Some compounds are written as one word (*earring*). Others are hyphenated (*forty-one*). Others are written as two or more words (*ice cream*).

Look at each compound word below. Leave it as is if the word does not need a hyphen or separation. Rewrite it if the word does need a hyphen or separation. Use a dictionary to make sure your answers are correct.

1. boxseat   box seat
2. mailbox   _____
3. timeout   _____
4. safetypin   safety pin
5. pogostick   pogo stick
6. printout   _____
7. showoff   show-off
8. fatherinlaw   father-in-law
9. photocopy   _____
10. motherofpearl   mother-of-pearl

Write sentences using compound nouns other than the ones listed above.

1. He wears a red armband.
2. What happened to your buttonhole?
3. There goes a double-decker bus.

© Carson-Dellosa CD-3744   3

Possessive Nouns

To make a singular noun **possessive**, add '-s. If the noun ends in -s and is plural in meaning, add only an apostrophe. If the noun is singular in meaning but ends in -s, add '-s. If a plural noun does not end in -s the possessive is formed by adding -'s.

<u>Noun not ending in s</u>	<u>Noun ending in s</u>	<u>Irregular Plurals</u>
the boy	the boys	children
the *boy's* baseball	the *boys'* baseball	*children's* toys
the boss	the bosses	
the *boss's* temper	the *bosses'* meeting	
Maxine		
Maxine's book		

The singular form of the noun is given. Write the other three forms.

Singular	Singular Possessive	Plural	Plural Possessive
book	*book's*	*books*	*books'*
1. tent	tent's	tents	tents'
2. shoe	shoe's	shoes	shoes'
3. tree	tree's	trees	trees'
4. violin	violin's	violins	violins'
5. story	story's	stories	stories'
6. raccoon	raccoon's	raccoons	raccoons'
7. picture	picture's	pictures	pictures'
8. tale	tale's	tales	tales'
9. cup	cup's	cups	cups'
10. calendar	calendar's	calendars	calendars'
11. baker	baker's	bakers	bakers'
12. pencil	pencil's	pencils	pencils'
13. boss	boss's	bosses	bosses'

© Carson-Dellosa CD-3744   4

Answer Pages

Name _____

Nouns

Possessive Nouns

The singular form of the noun is given. Write the other forms requested.

Singular	Singular Possessive	Plural	Plural Possessive
book	book's	books	books'
1. machine	machine's	machines	machines'
2. horse	horse's	horses	horses'
3. daffodil	daffodil's	daffodils	daffodils'
4. beach	beach's	beaches	beaches'
5. chair	chair's	chairs	chairs'
6. dancer	dancer's	dancers	dancers'
7. novel	novel's	novels	novels'
8. postcard	postcard's	postcards	postcards'
9. airplane	airplane's	airplanes	airplanes'
10. musical	musical's	musicals	musicals'
11. chef	chef's	chefs	chefs'
12. paper	paper's	papers	papers'
13. class	class's	classes	classes'
14. couch	couch's	couches	couches'
15. pencil	pencil's	pencils	pencils'

Nouns

Nouns Functioning as Subjects

Nouns and pronouns can function as the subject of the sentence. To decide if a word is the subject, ask *who* or *what* followed by the verb. The noun is called the simple subject. The subject usually precedes the verb, but not always.

Example: <u>Mary</u> runs five miles daily.
The tall, blonde <u>runner</u> is going to the Olympics.
A <u>competition</u> is always held in the spring.

Underline the noun that is the subject in each sentence.

1. <u>Salvador</u> went on a whale watching tour out of Half Moon Bay in California.
2. The <u>weather</u> was cold and windy.
3. The <u>passengers</u> on the boat waved good-bye.
4. The tour <u>guide</u> explained the migratory habits of grey whales.
5. The selected <u>area</u> for viewing was about one hour from shore.
6. The cold, rough <u>winds</u> made the trip rather uncomfortable.
7. Many <u>people</u> got seasick.
8. After no sightings for two hours, the <u>captain</u> decided to return to shore.
9. Most <u>people</u> were terribly disappointed.
10. The seasick <u>people</u> were not disappointed when they turned back toward the shore.
11. Suddenly, three <u>whales</u> were spotted together.
12. The immense <u>mammals</u> rose powerfully out of the water over and over.
13. The <u>tourists</u> were mesmerized by their encounter.
14. Even the most seasick <u>woman</u> managed to get a good look.
15. During the return to shore the marine <u>biologist</u> talked very seriously about endangered species such as these.

Nouns

Nouns as Simple Subjects and Noun Phrases as Complete Subjects

Nouns and pronouns can function as the subject of the sentence. To decide if a word is the subject, ask *who* or *what* followed by the verb. A noun without its modifiers is called the **simple subject**. A noun with its modifiers is called a noun phrase and becomes the **complete subject**. Noun phrases include adjectives, adverbs that intensify the adjectives, and prepositional phrases. They extend and complete the noun's meaning in various ways.

Example: <u>Mary</u> runs five miles daily. (simple subject)
The tall, girl in the blue shorts is going to the Olympics. (complete subject)

Underline the simple subject in each sentence. Circle the complete subject.

1. The moonless, brisk <u>night</u> was perfect for Halloween.
2. The howling <u>wind</u> added to the effect.
3. Hooting <u>owls</u> could be heard in the treetops.
4. Wild-eyed black <u>cats</u> roamed through the streets.
5. Scary yard <u>decorations</u> were evident everywhere.
6. The excited <u>children</u> in their scary costumes ran from house to house.
7. A <u>boy</u> in a mummy costume had the largest bag for treats.
8. A <u>vampire</u> with glistening fangs walked beside him.
9. The cackling <u>laughter</u> of a tall witch made them scatter.
10. The triumphant <u>witch</u> watched the two boys run for the safety of a porch.
11. Two cute little <u>skeletons</u> knocked on Mr. Burke's door.
12. A <u>ghost</u> in a white sheet opened the door.
13. Homemade <u>cookies</u> in orange trick-or-treat bags were given to each child.
14. A prissy <u>ballerina</u> in a pink tutu walked by with her mother and a werewolf.
15. Laughing <u>children</u> ran from house to house with their bags of treats.

Nouns

Nouns Functioning as Predicate Nominatives

The **predicate nominative** is a noun or pronoun that follows a linking verb and renames or gives more information about the subject. It answers the question *Who* or *What is*. The linking verb describes a condition, not an action. The most common linking verb is *to be* in its various forms (*am, is, was,* and *were*) as well as *to become*.

Example: Langston Hughes was a great <u>poet</u>.

Read the sentence. Underline the predicate nominative once. Underline the linking verb twice. Draw an arrow from the predicate nominative to the subject it renames. If there is no predicate nominative, skip the sentence.

1. Jody's pet in Rawling's novel *The Yearling* <u>is</u> a playful and affectionate young <u>deer</u>.
2. The woman at the center of controversy in *The Tales of King Arthur* <u>was</u> <u>Guinevere</u>.
3. *The Outsiders* by S.E. Hinton <u>is</u> a dramatic <u>novel</u> for young teens narrated by a character named Ponyboy.
4. Charles Dickens <u>is</u> the <u>author</u> of the classic favorite *Oliver Twist*.
5. Beth is currently reading *The Little Prince*.
6. George Orwell's *Animal Farm* <u>is</u> an <u>allegory</u> that uses farm animals to illustrate the dangers of totalitarian government.
7. The Newbery Medal is awarded to the best piece of children's literature every year.
8. *The Old Man and the Sea* by Ernest Hemingway <u>is</u> a deceptively simple <u>story</u> of an old man's battle with a giant marlin.
9. The main character in Tolkein's *The Hobbit* <u>is</u> a far-wandering <u>creature</u> named Bilbo Baggins.
10. Homer's story of the Trojan War, *The Iliad*, has <u>been</u> a <u>fixture</u> in libraries and book stores all over the world for many years.
11. *Alice's Adventures in Wonderland, Through the Looking Glass,* and *What Alice Found There* were all written by Lewis Carroll.
12. *Death Be Not Proud* <u>is</u> a beautifully written <u>memoir</u> by John Gunther about his son.

Answer Pages

Name _____ Nouns

Nouns Functioning as Direct Objects

A noun (or pronoun) used as a **direct object** tells *who* or *what* receives the action of the verb. A verb can have more than one direct object.

Example: I saw the Marie.
John saw the movie and its sequel.

Underline the direct object in each sentence. Circle the verb. Leave the sentence blank if there is no direct object.

1. Betty recently (toured) Australia.
2. A big highlight of the trip for her was the colony of fairy penguins on Phillips Island.
3. On the way from Melbourne to Phillips Island, she (had) parsnip soup for lunch at a delightful farm.
4. Betty (fed) bread to kangaroos and a peacock there.
5. She also (met) an unforgettable wombat at the farm.
6. Betty next (visited) the Koala Conservation Center on the island.
7. She could (reach) the lower treetops by means of ramps for better viewing of koalas.
8. Luckily, she did not (see) the local ten foot worm that also lived in the conservation center.
9. Betty (saw) her first fairy penguin at Nobby's Point.
10. This 17"-tall penguin (had) a beautiful bluish back and a white belly.
11. She (saw) many fairy penguins coming out of the sea in groups of three to twenty-five.
12. Many of them were (carrying) fish back to their mates on land.
13. Betty could actually (see) the females patting their returning mates in apparent appreciation for the meal.
14. At dinner that night she (saw) a picture of a 21' shark that was captured right off Nobby's Point.

9

Name _____ Nouns

Nouns Functioning as Indirect Objects

A noun (or pronoun) that tells *to whom* or *for whom* the action of the verb is done is called the **indirect object**. One verb may refer to more than one indirect object. A sentence containing an indirect object must also contain a direct object.

Example: I gave Sally a dollar. (direct object—dollar; indirect object—Sally)
I gave Sally and her sister a ride to school. (direct object—ride; indirect objects—Sally and sister)

Underline the indirect object(s) in each sentence. Circle the verb. Underline the direct object twice.

1. Marcy (gave) her teacher a bouquet of flowers.
2. Aunt Alice (sends) Drew a birthday present every year.
3. My teacher (taught) the class facts about solar energy today.
4. Ben Franklin High School (offers) its students a strong college prep curriculum.
5. I (told) my youngest sister a bedtime story.
6. Beverly (showed) her best friend a picture of her new love.
7. Alex (told) Roxanne a big secret.
8. Every summer the Smiths (send) their daughter a box of goodies at her camp.
9. The professor (taught) his students French.
10. Alice (wrote) her pen pal a detailed letter every month.
11. Joseph (bought) his fiancee a diamond engagement ring.
12. Patricia (showed) the producers her considerable talent at the audition.
13. Robert (refused) Milly her request.
14. The drunken pirate (showed) the young boy a treasure map.
15. The wealthy man (showed) the beggar some unaccustomed kindness.

10

Name _____ Nouns

Nouns Functioning as Objects of Prepositions

A noun (or pronoun) or noun phrase often follows a preposition to form a prepositional phrase. The **preposition** shows relationships between the noun and some other words in the sentence. The noun is called the object of the preposition. Some of the most common prepositions include *about, across, around, at, before, between, by, down, during, for, from, inside, into, of, on, over, under,* and *with*.

Example: Albany is the capital of New York. (shows relationship of capital to *New York*)
The cat ran under the bed. (shows relationship of ran to *bed*)

Circle each preposition. Underline each object of the preposition.

1. She speaks (with) a lovely French accent.
2. (On) the top shelf you will find the psychology books.
3. The mail arrives (at) approximately four o'clock.
4. She stood stubbornly (at) the door.
5. The Miller family lives (in) the suburbs (of) Los Angeles.
6. The new teacher is (from) the state (of) Utah.
7. I can't travel (during) the summer.
8. We will leave (at) midnight.
9. Wait (until) dark.
10. The owner's manual comes (with) the computer.
11. The hurricane is moving (across) the Atlantic seacoast.
12. Valerie lives across the street (in) the red brick house.
13. Michelle is (from) a small town (in) France.
14. During the intermission we stood (on) the balcony (of) the theater.
15. I left my homework (on) my desk (at) home.
16. The accident resulted (in) a broken leg.

11

Name _____ Nouns

Nouns Functioning as Appositives

An **appositive** is a type of noun or noun phrase that identifies the same person or object by another name. It is usually enclosed in commas and immediately follows the noun it identifies. It renames the subject or predicate nominative. If the first noun is unclear without the help of the appositive, commas are not used.

Example: Julie, a great dancer, got the role of the Sugar Plum Fairy.
My friend Anais got the role of Clara.

Read the two sentences. Underline the part in the second sentence which can be used to expand the first sentence. Rewrite the first sentence so that it has an appositive when expanded.

Example: 1. Julie got the role of the Sugar Plum Fairy.
Julie is a great dancer.
Julie, a great dancer, got the role of the Sugar Plum Fairy.

2. My friend got the role of Clara.
My friend is Anais.
My friend Anais got the role of Clara.

1. Ms. Sharon Ramsey is our choice for senator.
Ms. Sharon Ramsey is a reform candidate.

   Ms. Sharon Ramsey, a reform candidate, is our choice for senator.
   _____

2. The United Nations is based in New York City.
The United Nations is the most influential international organization.

   The United Nations, the most influential international organization, is based in New York City.

3. Mark just made a remarkable discovery in the Andes Mountains.
Mark is a paleontologist.

   Mark, a paleontologist, just made a remarkable discovery in the Andes Mountains.

12

Answer Pages

Nouns Functioning as Appositives

Read the two sentences. Underline the part in the second sentence which can be used to expand the first sentence. Rewrite the first sentence so that it has an appositive when expanded.

Example: Julie got the role of the Sugar Plum Fairy.
            Julie is a great dancer.
            Julie, a great dancer, got the role of the Sugar Plum Fairy.

1. The car was vandalized in the parking lot.
   The car was <u>a luxury convertible</u>.
   The car, a luxury convertible, was vandalized in the parking lot.

2. Carla designed the itinerary for our trip to Alaska.
   Carla is <u>a very experienced travel consultant</u>.
   Carla, a very experienced travel consultant, designed the itinerary for our trip to Alaska.

3. Mary Shelley's novel is a great classic tale of horror.
   Mary Shelley's novel is <u>Frankenstein</u>.
   Mary Shelley's novel Frankenstein is a great classic tale of horror.

4. The word was misused in this sentence.
   The word is <u>disinterested</u>.
   The word disinterested was misused in this sentence.

5. Agoraphobia often affects depressed women.
   Agoraphobia is <u>the fear of being in open spaces</u>.
   Agoraphobia, the fear of being in open spaces, often affects depressed women.

Noun Functions Review

Look at the underlined noun. Decide its function in the sentence. Write S for subject, DO for direct object, IO for indirect object, PN for predicate nominative, OP for object of the preposition, or A for appositive.

S 1. Julie Andrews' remarkable <u>voice</u> was first discovered when she was nine years old.

OP 2. She came from a family with a theatrical <u>background</u> in the English Music Hall tradition, although no one before her achieved Julie's level of success.

IO 3. At the age of thirteen, Julie gave the royal <u>family</u> a solo performance in London.

DO 4. At 23, she crossed the <u>Atlantic</u> in order to pursue a career on Broadway.

PN 5. Her first theatrical smash hit was <u>My Fair Lady</u>.

PN 6. Her co-star in *My Fair Lady* was <u>Rex Harrison</u>.

PN 7. Her most famous movie role was probably <u>Maria</u> in *The Sound of Music*.

OP 8. *The Sound of Music* made Julie a household name all over the <u>world</u>.

S 9. *The Sound of Music* was based on the true story of a famous Austrian woman and the events in her life at the beginning of World War II.

PN 10. The pinnacle of Julie's movie career thus far would probably be her <u>Oscar</u> for best actress in the movie *Mary Poppins*.

OP 11. One of her funniest <u>performances</u> was in *Victoria, Victoria*.

S 12. <u>Julie</u> starred in *Victor, Victoria* both in the movie and on Broadway.

OP 13. Julie herself was particularly fond of her <u>role</u> as Guinivere in the musical *Camelot*.

DO 14. Her live performances always demonstrate the full <u>range</u> of her vocal and acting abilities.

PN 15. Additionally, she is the <u>author</u> of a popular children's novel called *Mandy* written under the name of Julie Edwards.

Noun Functions Review

Look at the underlined noun. Decide its function in the sentence. Write S for subject, DO for direct object, IO for indirect object, PN for predicate nominative, OP for object of the preposition, or A for appositive.

The Eastern and Oriental Express

The Eastern and Oriental Express, called the E & O, is a luxurious Asian <u>train</u> that goes ¹ from <u>Bangkok</u> to Singapore. The <u>train</u> is a deluxe railway <u>experience</u>, and there are few of ² ³ ⁴ these left in the world today.

Although it was built in Japan in 1971, its <u>style</u> is purposefully reminiscent of the ⁵ 1930's. The forest green and yellow E & O contains a <u>locomotive</u> and eighteen <u>carriages</u>. ⁶ ⁷ The luxurious <u>interior</u> is designed for first-class rail <u>travel</u>. The <u>train</u> has an open obser- ⁸ ⁹ ¹⁰ vation deck, a lavish formal dining car, some sleeper suites paneled in cherry wood and elm burl, and a pale ash-paneled lounge car complete with <u>piano</u>. ¹¹

The train leaves Bangkok, Thailand and soon the <u>temples</u> mixed with <u>skyscrapers</u> are ¹² ¹³ left behind. A watery <u>landscape</u> with only occasional teak <u>houses</u> follows. On the second ¹⁴ ¹⁵ day, the train is in <u>Malaysia</u>, and the <u>scenery</u> changes to tidy <u>villages</u> and water buffalo. ¹⁶ ¹⁷ ¹⁸ The passengers get off the train briefly at Penang Island. Here they get to ride in a <u>trishaw</u>, a three-wheeled vehicle, that is propelled by a pedaling driver. ¹⁹ The train then starts ascending as it heads into the mountainous highland region of Malaysia. <u>Rainforests</u> filled with <u>monkeys</u> narrowly line the <u>train</u>. The <u>passengers</u> take a ²⁰ ²¹ ²² ²³ 30-minute midnight stop in Kuala Lumpur, the capital of <u>Malaysia</u>. Finally, two days later, ²⁴ the train pulls into the <u>station</u> in Singapore.

1. PN	6. DO	11. OP	16. OP	21. OP
2. OP	7. DO	12. S	17. S	22. DO
3. S	8. S	13. OP	18. OP	23. S
4. PN	9. OP	14. S	19. OP	24. OP
5. S	10. S	15. OP	20. S	25. OP

Personal, Indefinite, and Demonstrative Pronouns

Pronouns take the place of nouns. Here are three kinds:
1. **Personal pronouns** include forms of first, second and third person: *I, mine, me, we, ours, us, you, yours, he, she, it, his, hers, its, him, her, they, theirs,* and *them*.
   Example: <u>They</u> are the best of friends.
2. **Indefinite pronouns** refer to persons or things generally. *Anybody, few, most, neither, no one, nothing,* and *several* are some indefinite pronouns.
   Example: <u>No one</u> said a word.
3. **Demonstrative pronouns** refer to persons or things specifically: *this, that, these,* and *those*.
   Example: Don't eat <u>those</u>.

Underline the pronoun used in each sentence. Identify it as P (personal), I (indefinite), or D (demonstrative).

I 1. Mary doesn't know anyone in the room.

P 2. You can't be serious.

P 3. He is out of the race.

P 4. My father doesn't trust them.

P 5. It won't staple.

P 6. Max will play chess with you.

I 7. Neither was prepared for the pop quiz.

P 8. They filled the stadium to watch the contending ice skaters.

D 9. The teacher won't recognize these.

P 10. Unless Beth goes, I won't.

D 11. These belong to Patrick.

I 12. Just a few won't hurt.

I 13. I brought several.

P 14. Brandy could see nothing in the dim light.

D 15. These are Joey's favorite cookies.

Answer Pages

Interrogative and Relative Pronouns

Interrogative pronouns are used to ask questions. **Relative pronouns** introduce dependent clauses in sentences. (A dependent clause contains a subject and verb, but does not stand alone as a complete thought.) Except for *that* which is relative, but not interrogative, these pronouns are identical in form. These pronouns include *who, whom, whoever, whomever, which, what, whatever,* and *whichever.*

    Example: <u>Who</u> is your first choice? (interrogative)
                The girl <u>who looks upset</u> is my sister. (relative pronoun in dependent clause)

If the underlined pronoun is interrogative, write I in the blank. If the underlined pronoun is relative write R in the blank. Underline the clause that goes with the relative pronoun.

  R   1. I will bring <u>whatever you request</u>.
  I   2. <u>Whatever</u> is the matter with you?
  I   3. <u>Which</u> essay won?
  R   4. The essay <u>which was written by Alyssa</u> won.
  R   5. Choose <u>whichever you want</u>.
  I   6. <u>What</u> is the title of that song?
  R   7. I don't know <u>what she said</u>.
  I   8. <u>Who</u> betrayed my confidence?
  R   9. I will always remember the nurse <u>who was so kind</u>.
  R 10. The child <u>whom I saw</u> was about five years old.
  I 11. <u>Whom</u> did you see at the parade?
  R 12. The person to <u>whom I gave my donation</u> is the director of the campaign.
  I 13. For <u>whom</u> is this gift intended?
  I 14. <u>Whoever</u> could be responsible for this problem?
  R 15. I will invite <u>whoever you like</u>.
  R 16. Melissa gets <u>whatever she wants</u>.
  I 17. <u>What</u> happened here?
  R 18. Do you know <u>what time it is</u>?
  I 19. <u>Who</u> was on the answering machine?
  R 20. I know to <u>whom the brooch belongs</u>.

Possessive Pronouns

The personal pronouns *mine, yours, his, hers, ours,* and *theirs* show possession. Apostrophes are not used with possessive pronouns as they are with possessive nouns.
    Example: That ice cream cone is <u>mine</u>.

The personal pronouns *my, your, her, its, our,* and *their* show possession, but are always followed by nouns.
    Example: That is <u>my</u> ice cream.

The personal pronoun *his* may or may not be followed by a noun.
    Example: That is <u>his</u> ice cream.
               That ice cream is <u>his</u>.

Write a possessive pronoun in each blank to complete the sentences. Circle any nouns that follow the possessive pronoun.

1. That wallet is _____his_____.
2. _____Her_____ (friend) is a salesclerk here.
3. I thought it was _____mine_____.
4. We gave the winner _____our_____ (approval.)
5. _____Your_____ (apology) is not accepted.
6. Is this jacket _____yours_____?
7. This is _____her_____ (jacket.)
8. My locker was locked, and I did not have _____my_____ (key.)
9. This is _____their_____ (room.)
10. The best disciplined dog in the show is _____ours_____.
11. _____His_____ (excuse) sounded pretty flimsy.
12. I'm sorry that I spilled coffee on _____your_____ (dress.)
13. We all took a long rest after _____our_____ exhaustive (ordeal.)
14. _____Her_____ (explanation) sounded reasonable.

Nominative and Objective Case in Pronouns

The case of a pronoun depends on its use in the sentence. The **nominative case** includes the subject, predicate nominative and appositive. The pronouns used in the nominative case include *I, you, he, she, it, we,* and *they.* The **objective case** includes the direct object, indirect object, and object of the preposition. The pronouns used in the objective case include *me, you, him, her, it, us,* and *them.*

    Example: <u>I</u> know <u>them</u>. (subject and direct object)
                Jeff gave <u>me</u> that letter. (indirect object)
                <u>It</u> was <u>I</u> who told the teacher. (subject and predicate nominative)
                The present was for <u>him</u>. (object of the preposition)

Circle the correct pronoun in the nominative or objective case. Write its function in the blank. Choose S for subject, PN for predicate nominative, A for appositive, DO for direct object, IO for indirect object, or OP for object of the preposition.

  S   1. One winter evening (we) us) went ice skating together.
  S   2. You and (she,) her) need to finish your homework.
 PN 3. Next year's student council president might be ((he) him).
 PN 4. Our best volleyball players are ((they) them).
 DO 5. Call (I, (me.)
 DO 6. Call (she, (her.)
  IO 7. We showed (they, (them) the treasure map.
 DO 8. The teacher watched (he, (him) hand out papers.
 DO 9. The bat hit (I, (me) right in the nose.
 DO 10. The usher escorted (they, (them) to the seats.
 OP 11. She sat next to Amy and (I, (me.)
 OP 12. We walked toward (they, (them.)
 OP 13. The traffic guard stopped and glared at Jake and (I, (me.)
  IO 14. I gave (he, (him) a slice of my homemade pecan pie.
 OP 15. Give the directions to (she, (her.)

Action Verbs

The verb states something about the subject. A verb that expresses action is called an **action verb.**

    Example: The snake <u>slithered</u> under the log.
                The snake <u>slithered</u> under the log, and then it <u>reappeared</u>.
                That snake has <u>startled</u> me for the last time! (an auxiliary verb can accompany the action verb)

Underline the action verb in each sentence. Circle the subject.

1. (Valerie) <u>loves</u> creative gardening.
2. The (search) for new additions to her garden <u>goes</u> on and on.
3. For instance, yesterday (she) <u>spotted</u> a wild aster in the brush of a vacant lot.
4. (She) gently <u>pulled</u> up the aster by its roots.
5. (Valerie) <u>tucked</u> the flower beside a fuzzy goldenrod in her side yard.
6. The whole (yard) is <u>brimming</u> with black-eyed susans, sunflowers, and honeysuckle.
7. A (pond) in the center is <u>filled</u> with water lilies and frogs.
8. Her (passion) for wildflowers is also <u>demonstrated</u> throughout her garden.
9. (She) has <u>transformed</u> her yard into a haven for the native flora and associated wildlife.
10. Her (choices) of plants <u>lure</u> birds, butterflies, and bugs with their nectar and berries.
11. (They) <u>offer</u> shelter with safe branches and scrubby brambles.
12. Every (plant) <u>grows</u> as if it has a special purpose.
13. (She) <u>reads</u> everything available on gardening.
14. Migratory (birds) and (mockingbirds) often <u>fly</u> through her little haven.
15. Residential (birds) like cardinals and bluejays <u>spend</u> their lives there.
16. A (bed) of bright flowers <u>attracts</u> butterflies and bees.
17. Wild (animals) are not the only animals <u>tempted</u> by the garden.
18. (Youngsters) <u>come</u> to Valerie's home for seeds and advice.
19. (People) from all over town <u>come</u> with thoughtful additions for her garden.
20. (They) proudly <u>watch</u> their contributions become part of Valerie's wonderful haven.

Answer Pages

Auxiliary Verbs

Auxiliary verbs, also called helping verbs, never occur without a main verb. An **auxiliary verb** helps the main verb to express tense, voice, or mood, but usually has little meaning of its own. Some examples include *be, do, have, can, might, would, may, will,* and *must.* Two or more verbs combined is called a verb phrase. Verb phrases contain at least one auxiliary verb. Adverbs may appear in the middle of a verb phrase, but they are not part of it.

    Example: We <u>are</u> waiting in a long line.
                I <u>would</u> have gone with him.
                I <u>could</u> hardly wait.

Underline the main verb once. Underline the auxiliary verb(s) twice.

1. The West Highland White Terrier <u>has attained</u> a high degree of popularity as both a loyal pet and a show dog.
2. Before this century, these hardy animals <u>had abounded</u> as working dogs in the Scottish Highlands for over three hundred years.
3. They <u>had earned</u> their livings following fox, badger, and otter for hunters.
4. The ancestors of the breed <u>were known</u> in the past under various names such as Roseneath and Little Skye.
5. The breed <u>was</u> first <u>classified</u> at the annual show of The Scottish Kennel Club in 1904.
6. After 1916, all shows <u>were stopped</u> by World War I.
7. Breeding <u>was prohibited</u> in 1917 and 1918, and no dogs <u>were allowed</u> to be registered.
8. By 1919 breeding <u>had started</u> again, and soon many dogs <u>were registered</u>.
9. A long line of champions <u>has followed</u>.
10. The breed <u>has been described</u> as linty white in color with hard and bristly hair.
11. The Westie should <u>have</u> a long stride, straight shoulders, and a stilted gait.
12. It <u>has been noted</u> for its attentive ears, free, cheerful movement, and high self-esteem.

Linking Verbs

Linking verbs describe conditions instead of actions. They are followed by words that rename or describe the subject. Forms of the verb *to be* are most commonly used as linking verbs, although these forms can also be used as auxiliary verbs in verb phrases. Other forms include *appear, become, feel, grow, look, prove, remain, seem* and *turn.* These verbs do not function as linking verbs if they do not describe conditions that are followed by a word that renames or describes the subject.

    Example: Carla <u>is</u> my only sister. (linking)
                Carla's friend <u>is</u> running for governor. (auxiliary)
                Bob <u>grew</u> sleepy during the long lecture. (linking)
                Roger <u>grew</u> beautiful roses in his garden. (action)

Look at each underlined verb. If the verb is linking, write L in the blank. If the verb is auxiliary write AUX in the blank. If it is an action verb write ACT in the blank.

  L   1. Matthew <u>is</u> a really tall fellow.
AUX 2. That puppy <u>is</u> following me again.
ACT 3. The gypsy <u>turned</u> the tarot card.
  L   4. She <u>turned</u> pale when she saw the ghost.
  L   5. Marsha <u>became</u> a grandmother at sixty-one.
  L   6. He <u>was</u> an Elvis look-alike.
ACT 7. Elizabeth <u>felt</u> a fever coming on.
  L   8. Jennifer <u>felt</u> a bit sheepish.
  L   9. The maple tree <u>is</u> a good spot for meditating.
AUX 10. The bee <u>was</u> circling my head.
AUX 11. His booksack <u>was</u> found in the gym.
  L   12. Her purse <u>looked</u> shabby.
ACT 13. The toddler <u>looked</u> under the bed.
  L   14. Mary and Ben <u>remained</u> friends for life.
ACT 15. The guilty person <u>remained</u> silent.

Principle Parts and Irregular Verbs

The principle parts of a verb are the three forms upon which all tenses are based.

Present	Past	Past Participle (uses has, have, or had)
love	loved	has, have, or had loved

Many frequently used verbs have principle parts that are irregularly formed.

Present	Past	Past Participle (uses has, have, or had)
drive	drove	has, have, or had driven

The present form of the verb has been given. Fill in the past and the past participle forms. Use a dictionary to check your work.

Present	Past	Past Participle
1. forget	forgot	have forgotten
2. respond	responded	have responded
3. teach	taught	have taught
4. forbid	forbade	have forbidden
5. sink	sank	have sunk
6. slip	slipped	have slipped
7. break	broke	have broken
8. freeze	froze	have frozen
9. talk	talked	have talked
10. throw	threw	have thrown
11. choose	chose	have chosen
12. stroll	strolled	have strolled
13. hear	heard	have heard
14. awake	awoke	have awoken
15. be	was/were	have been
16. eat	ate	have eaten
17. allow	allowed	have allowed
18. ride	rode	have ridden

Principle Parts of Verbs

The principle parts of a verb are the three forms upon which all tenses are based.

Present	Past	Past Participle (uses has, have, or had)
love	loved	has, have, or had loved

Many frequently used verbs have principle parts that are irregularly formed.

Present	Past	Past Participle (uses has, have, or had)
drive	drove	has, have, or had driven

Write the verb form that is asked for in each of the following sentences. (P is for past and PP is for past participle). Additional auxiliary verbs may be used.

1. The news of the assassination **had been broadcast** around the world within minutes of its occurrence. (PP of *broadcast*)
2. Allison **has become** obsessed with losing weight in the past few months. (PP of *become*)
3. The baby **cried** in the middle of the night. (P of *cry*)
4. The teller was found after the robbery with his hands **bound**. (P of *bind*)
5. Patricia **had chosen** the perfect dress for her school's Spring Formal. (PP of *choose*)
6. The fire **burned** out of control very quickly. (P of *burn*)
7. He **bent** the metal bar with his bare hands. (P of *bend*)
8. The principal **had instructed** the unruly student to come to his office after school. (PP of *instruct*)
9. The aggressive dog **had bitten** the unsuspecting boy on the leg. (PP of *bite*)
10. Kristin **bought** a large pack of indelible markers. (P of *buy*)
11. The clock **had crept** along for hours as Tom tossed and turned. (PP of *creep*)
12. The child **hid** behind the heavy, brocade curtains. (P of *hide*)

Answer Pages

Name _____ **Verbs**

Simple Verb Tenses

The tense of the verb shows the time of an action. The **simple present tense** shows that an action takes place now at the same time that it is being described. It is also used to describe habitual action, to tell general truths, and to write about books, movies and other narratives. It can also be used to indicate a time in the future. The **past tense** shows that an action took place at some previous time. The **future tense** shows the action will take place at some time to come.

Examples: The child <u>fills</u> her dog's bowl daily with fresh water. (present, habitual action)
The people <u>elect</u> their government in a democratic society. (present, general truths)
I <u>leave</u> for Costa Rica tomorrow. (present, describing time in future)
He <u>filled</u> the glasses and everyone toasted. (past)
Jenny <u>will fill</u> the garden with bright annuals. (future)

Underline the complete verb. Determine the tense. Write PR for present, PT for past, or F for future on the line provided.

_PT_ 1. The feisty, young cat scratched the brand new wallpaper with his claws.

_F_ 2. I will prune the roses tomorrow.

_PR_ 3. You know the answer to that question.

_PT_ 4. Mrs. Schon left the country for several months to live in a warmer climate.

_PR_ 5. *The Little Prince* by Antoine de Saint-Exupery is an enchanting fable filled with hidden truths.

_F_ 6. Meg will bake sugar cookies with colorful sprinkles for the Christmas party.

_PT_ 7. Mother gave each of her daughters a cashmere sweater for their birthdays.

_PT_ 8. Drew yawned enormously.

_PR_ 9. The new movie features an outstanding cast of talented young actresses.

_PR_ 10. In your opinion, is the most exciting city in the United States New York or Los Angeles?

_PT_ 11. The recipe for vegetarian lasagna was on the back of the package of pasta.

_PT_ 12. She gave us a shy smile.

_F_ 13. Will you be dining with us this evening?

_PR_ 14. How old is the child in this play?

© Carson-Dellosa CD-3744   25

Name _____ **Verbs**

Simple Past Tense

Rewrite each sentence below in the simple past tense.

1. I find that story very amusing.
   I found that story very amusing.

2. The bird chirps on my window sill every morning.
   The bird chirped on my window sill every morning.

3. The scissors cut very poorly.
   The scissors cut very poorly.

4. Jan will sell her jewelry at the flea market.
   Jan sold her jewelry at the flea market.

5. Mother fixes a balanced lunch for each of her children to take to school.
   Mother fixed a balanced lunch for each of her children to take to school.

6. Sarah will tell a scary tale around the campfire.
   Sarah told a scary tale around the campfire.

7. Patty always insists on seeing the positive side of a situation.
   Patty always insisted on seeing the positive side of a situation.

8. Patrick will ride in the Kentucky Derby.
   Patrick rode in the Kentucky Derby.

9. The pages tear easily.
   The pages tore easily.

10. The audience laughs at every line.
    The audience laughed at every line.

© Carson-Dellosa CD-3744   26

Name _____ **Verbs**

Simple Past Tense

Supply a past tense verb to complete each sentence below.

1. I ___ran___ a mile in six minutes and ten seconds.
2. Esther ___polished___ the silver until it gleamed.
3. You ___played___ without looking at the keys.
4. Myra ___wore___ a dress of pale blue silk.
5. Mr. Frazier ___sat___ in his favorite old chair.
6. Christopher ___finished___ his science project on Wednesday.
7. Mrs. Temple ___hid___ her money in an old coffee can.
8. Both of us ___cried___ until we fell asleep.
9. Al ___swam___ through the strong current.
10. We ___talked___ to the class about plagiarism.
11. You ___sold___ your stock for ten cents on the dollar.
12. Mr. Blake ___spent___ his holiday in Kansas visiting relatives.
13. None of us ___stole___ fifty dollars from the cash register.
14. The crystal glass ___broke___ on the hard tile floor.
15. Too many of you ___ate___ incredibly fatty food.
16. The ice cream ___melted___ in the heat.
17. Shelley ___spilled___ the whole box of pencils all over the floor.
18. Jack and I ___ran___ across the street after dinner.
19. Vicki ___cooked___ delectable spinach and oyster soup.
20. Linda ___forgot___ her purse on a table in the library.

©Kelley Wingate CD-3744   27

Name _____ **Verbs**

Simple Present Tense

Supply a present tense verb in each sentence below.

1. The principal ___likes___ my parents very well.
2. We ___sing___ whenever we get the chance.
3. The dog ___barks___ at everything that moves.
4. I ___check___ the mail every evening.
5. The yacht ___leaves___ in a few hours.
6. The bus usually ___arrives___ on schedule.
7. The recipe does not ___contain___ enough detail.
8. The door ___opens___ whenever the wind blows.
9. The dictionary ___has___ more information than just definitions.
10. The play ___opens___ next weekend.
11. The toddler ___treats___ the puppy like her rag doll.
12. The movie ___shows___ a lot of action.
13. The crown ___is___ not actually made of precious stones.
14. Mary and I ___wash___ the dishes to help his mother.
15. You should ___go___ to the doctor for an annual check-up.
16. Both of you ___spend___ a lot of money on shoes.
17. Our family ___wants___ a bright red convertible.
18. Madeline ___wears___ pink lipstick.
19. The detective ___follows___ every lead.
20. You two ___hide___ when she appears.

© Carson-Dellosa CD-3744   28

© Carson-Dellosa CD-3744   105

Answer Pages

Name _____ Verbs

Simple Present Tense

Rewrite each sentence in the simple present tense.

1. Betsy went to the park without me.
   Betsy goes to the park without me.
2. Mr. Avery will go to Hong Kong in the spring.
   Mr. Avery goes to Hong Kong in the Spring.
3. Sharon ate chocolate quite frequently.
   Sharon eats chocolate quite frequently.
4. The emergency room staff awaited the unexpected.
   The emergency room staff awaits the unexpected.
5. The tutor will help with reducing fractions.
   The tutor helps with reducing fractions.
6. Melody knew the name of that tune.
   Melody knows the name of that tune.
7. That lamb will follow her to school every day.
   That lamb follows her to school every day.
8. Alex read himself to sleep every night.
   Alex reads himself to sleep every night.
9. To the delight of her fans, the singer will arrive this afternoon.
   To the delight of her fans, the singer arrives this afternoon.
10. Michael loved to paint colorful sunsets.

Name _____ Verbs

Simple Future Tense

Rewrite each sentence in the simple future tense.

1. Valerie bought a new dress to wear to the opera.
   Valerie will buy a new dress to wear to the opera.
2. The instructor teaches young campers to swim.
   The instructor will teach young campers to swim.
3. I tried very hard to meet the deadline.
   I will try very hard to meet the deadline.
4. The cookies baked in ten minutes.
   The cookies will bake in ten minutes.
5. The star member of the basketball team gets a lot of publicity.
   The star member of the basketball team will get a lot of publicity.
6. The photographer took school pictures in October.
   The photographer will take school pictures in October.
7. This type of toy breaks easily.
   This type of toy will break easily.
8. The sculpture was displayed in front of City Hall.
   The sculpture will be displayed in front of city hall.
9. That car was used in the parade.
   That car will be used in the parade.
10. Roberta appeared on a local television program this week.
    Roberta will appear on a local television program.

Name _____ Verbs

Simple Future Tense

Rewrite each sentence in the simple future tense.

1. I finished my homework after dinner.
   I will finish my homework after dinner.
2. The toddler tore the pretty picture book.
   The toddler will tear the pretty picture book.
3. The plane departs at twelve noon.
   The plane will depart at twelve noon.
4. Alexander had to take another aspirin.
   Alexander will have to take another aspirin.
5. The travel agent held the reservation for twenty-four hours.
   The travel agent will hold the reservation for twenty-four hours.
6. The president gave a televised speech on the economy.
   The president will give a televised speech on the economy.
7. Barbara called me about the matter.
   Barbara will call me about the matter.
8. Margaret visited Ireland in October.
   Margaret will visit Ireland in October.
9. The Smith family got to skate at the rink in Central Park.
   The Smith family will get to skate at the rink in Central Park.
10. Did you tell me the whole truth?
    Will you tell me the whole truth?

Name _____ Verbs

Past Perfect Tense

The **past perfect tense** describes an event in the past in relation to another event in the past. It shows that an action was completed before another action in the past, or completed before a definite time. The past perfect tense uses *had* and the past participle form of the main verb.

Example: She had jogged for twenty minutes before she began to feel faint.
The Smiths had been married for ten years before their first child was born.

Fill in the blank using the past perfect form of the verb.

1. (learn) During the summer vacation Roger _____had learned_____ wilderness survival skills.
2. (eat) The children _____had eaten_____ pizza after three hours of bowling.
3. (consider) I acted before I _____had considered_____ the consequences.
4. (finish) Beth _____had finished_____ reading before the rest of us started.
5. (drive) Patricia _____had driven_____ over three hundred miles yesterday.
6. (sing) Myra _____had sung_____ that aria several times in her career.
7. (take) The rehearsal _____had taken_____ more time than expected.
8. (slip) Her ring _____had slipped_____ from her finger when she washed her hands.
9. (howl) The wind _____had howled_____ all through the night.
10. (choose) They _____had chosen_____ a place for the honeymoon before they called off their wedding.
11. (look) His candidacy for mayor _____had looked_____ good until the scandal was publicized.
12. (love) The benevolent king _____had loved_____ his loyal subjects for many years.

Answer Pages

Panel 1

Name _____ Verbs

Past Perfect Tense

Create a sentence using the past perfect tense of each given verb.

1. (kiss) I had kissed him good night before he left.

2. (announce) We had announced his arrival three times.

3. (break) Jane had broken the vase then her mother walked in.

4. (challenge) You had challenged her to a game of Chess.

5. (release) We had released the report before he walked in.

6. (wear) I had worn it so many times that it fell apart.

7. (tear) We had torn the picture so we had another one made.

8. (study) I had studied for many hours until she arrived.

9. (take) Jane had taken my pencil so I got another one.

10. (bark) If the dog had barked I would have heard it.

© Carson-Dellosa CD-3744   33

Panel 2

Name _____ Verbs

Present Perfect Tense

The **present perfect tense** describes an event that started in the past and continues to be the same in the present. It uses either *has* or *have plus* the past participle form of the verb and.

Example : He <u>has known</u> her for ten years.
We <u>have seen</u> the play several times.

Write the present perfect form of the verb in each blank.

1. (frighten) That old scarecrow ___has frightened___ crows from the cornfield for years.
2. (bake) Melanie's mother ___has baked___ six dozen cookies for the fund raiser.
3. (trap) The cat ___has trapped___ the mouse in the corner.
4. (visit) Those volunteers ___have visited___ the nursing home every Sunday.
5. (buy) I ___have bought___ a new notebook for biology.
6. (read) John ___has read___ Treasure Island more than once.
7. (hold) I ___have held___ your heavy suitcase for hours.
8. (write) Pamela ___has written___ a letter to the president.
9. (work) Cedric ___has worked___ on the computer all afternoon.
10. (bring) Who ___has brought___ a donation for the United Way?
11. (draw) Ms. Louis ___has drawn___ interesting caricatures for years.
12. (fall) The picture ___has fallen___ from the wall again.
13. (is) There ___has been___ a gloomy atmosphere around here all afternoon.
14. (follow) Penny ___has followed___ the rules.
15. (run) Your time ___has run___ out.

© Carson-Dellosa CD-3744   34

Panel 3

Name _____ Verbs

Present Perfect Tense

Read each sentence then underline the verb. Write in the blank if the tense is simple present (PR), simple past (PT), or simple future (F). Rewrite the sentence in the present perfect tense.

_PT_ 1. The mahogany table <u>was scratched.</u> The mahogany table has been scratched.

_F_ 2. Mr. Anderson <u>will change</u> jobs this year. Mr. Anderson has changed jobs this year.

_PT_ 3. The kicker <u>scored</u> nine points. The kicker has scored nine points.

_PR_ 4. Marcia often <u>cries</u> crocodile tears. Marcia has often cried crocodile tears.

_PT_ 5. Emily <u>dreamed</u> of finding pirate's loot. Emily has dreamed of finding pirate's loot.

_F_ 6. That company <u>will send</u> me a sample of its product. That company has sent me a sample of its product.

_PT_ 7. Jennifer <u>left</u> a message on the answer phone. Jennifer has left a message on the answer phone.

_PT_ 8. Mr. Moore <u>worked</u> for that firm for years. Mr. Moore has worked for that firm for years.

_F_ 9. They <u>will spend</u> years on that research project. They have spent years on that research project.

_PR_ 10. Chris always <u>knows</u> the latest gossip. Chris has always known the latest gossip.

© Carson-Dellosa CD-3744   35

Panel 4

Name _____ Verbs

Future Perfect Tense

The **future perfect tense** shows that an action will happen after something else in the future. It uses *will* (or *shall* with first person), *has* or *have*, and the past participle form of the verb.

Example: He <u>will have surrendered</u> by that time.
I <u>will have completed</u> the painting by Tuesday.

Supply a future perfect tense verb to complete each sentence below.

1. I ___will have met___ you by twelve o'clock.

2. The exam grades ___will have been___ on the classroom door for two hours before the building closes.

3. My father ___will have bought___ a new van in the spring.

4. Beth's mother ___will have made___ all of the costumes for the play by the afternoon of dress rehearsal.

5. The company ___will have shown___ a profit for the first time this year.

6. You ___will have left___ by the time he gets here.

7. I ___will have worn___ my new jeans for two days when I wash them.

8. Jane ___will have decorated___ her room before the week ends.

9. Mr. Sullivan's friends ___will have given___ him a surprise birthday party the Saturday before his fiftieth birthday.

10. The mallard ducks ___will have moved___ to this area by the time winter comes.

© Carson-Dellosa CD-3744   36

© Carson-Dellosa CD-3744   107

Answer Pages

Page 37

Name _____   **Verbs**

Future Perfect Tense

Look at the given verb. Create a sentence in the future perfect tense using each verb.

1. (learn) We will have learned a lot today.

2. (make) You will have made a lot of money this year.

3. (see) My mother will have seen me in the play after tomorrow.

4. (try) Nick will have tried this recipe before he goes to sleep.

5. (hop) I will have hopped a total of three miles when I am done.

6. (throw) Frank will have thrown the ball over three hundred yards by the end of the game.

7. (write) I will have written six letters to my grandmother by next month.

8. (play) Mike and Henry will have played that song three times before Jan starts to sing it.

9. (forget) You will have forgotten all that you have learned by then.

10. (bought) We will have bought fifteen cars in our lifetime.

© Carson-Dellosa CD-3744   37

Page 38

Name _____   **Verbs**

Progressive Form of a Verb

The **progressive form** of a verb indicates continuous or habitual action, or an event in progress. It is formed by adding -ing to a main verb (the present participle) that is preceded by an auxiliary verb.

Example:

	simple	progressive
present:	tell	is telling
past:	told	was telling
future:	will tell	will be telling

Underline the simple verb in each sentence. Rewrite each simple verb in the progressive form.

1. The puppy digs holes in the back yard.
   The puppy is digging holes in the back yard.

2. The airlines will start a fare war this month.
   The airlines will be starting a fare war this month.

3. Mr. Allen rewards his children for good report cards.
   Mr. allen is rewarding his children for good report cards.

4. The robber fled the scene of the crime.
   The robbers were fleeing the scene of the crime.

5. The children sell lemonade in the summer to make money.
   The children are selling lemonade in the summer to make money.

6. His words broke my heart.
   His words were breaking my heart.

7. The package arrives tomorrow.
   The package is arriving tomorrow.

8. The mothers will sew all of the costumes for the class play.
   The mothers will be sewing all of the costumes for the class play.

© Carson-Dellosa CD-3744   38

Page 39

Name _____   **Verbs**

Verb Tense Review

Underline the complete verb in each sentence. Select the letter of the verb tense it uses and write it on the line provided.

A) simple present	D) present perfect	G) present progressive
B) simple past	E) past perfect	H) past progressive
C) simple future	F) future perfect	I) future progressive

A   1. Patricia has found the treasure map.

B   2. The weather was hot and humid.

D   3. Mr. Mitchell has finally discovered the solution to his problem.

I   4. Will you be attending the graduation ceremony?

H   5. The robber was running from the scene of the crime.

A   6. I am responsible for the entire matter.

B   7. The dancers froze at that instant.

C   8. I will give serious thought to your proposal.

A   9. Find my car keys, please.

B   10. The computer was not turned off all night.

H   11. I was trying to reach you on your car phone this afternoon.

E   12. Many bald eagles have been spotted in Montana lately.

A   13. Polly has a peanut butter and banana sandwich for lunch.

A   14. That calendar is out-of-date.

G   15. You are trying your best.

© Carson-Dellosa CD-3744   39

Page 40

Name _____   **Verbs**

Verb Tense Review

Underline the complete verb in each sentence. Write its tense on the line provided.

A) simple present	D) present perfect	G) present progressive
B) simple past	E) past perfect	H) past progressive
C) simple future	F) future perfect	I) future progressive

Change the sentence to the tense requested and make any adjustments necessary.

Example: He ran to the store.   He was running to the store.
             simple past   past progressive

G   1. Ms. Wilson is running for lieutenant governor. (simple future)
   Ms. Wilson will run for lieutenant governor.

A   2. I get tired easily. (present progressive)
   I am getting tired easily.

B   3. The decision was made in haste. (present perfect)
   The decision has been made in haste.

B   4. Max drove all day. (future progressive)
   Max will be driving all day.

G   5. The baby is crying in her crib. (past progressive)
   The baby was crying in her crib.

A   6. Milly tells the truth. (past perfect)
   Milly had told the truth.

D   7. Dan has read that novel. (past)
   Dan read that novel.

B   8. Wendell taped the program. (future perfect)
   Wendell will have taped this program.

C   9. Jane will change her mind. (simple past)
   Jane changed her mind.

B   10. We danced all night. (future perfect)
   We will have danced all night.

© Carson-Dellosa CD-3744   40

Answer Pages

Name _____   **Verbs**

Verb Tense Review

Underline the complete verb in each sentence. Write its tense on the line provided.

A) simple present	D) present perfect	G) present progressive
B) simple past	E) past perfect	H) past progressive
C) simple future	F) future perfect	I) future progressive

Change the sentence to the tense requested and make any adjustments necessary.

Example: He <u>ran</u> to the store.   He <u>was running</u> to the store.
           simple past   past progressive

__I__ 1. Jane <u>will be attending</u> the conference. (simple future)

Jane will attend the conference.

__B__ 2. Sam <u>found</u> the history test difficult. (present progressive)

Sam is finding the history test difficult.

__B__ 3. Marius <u>fell</u> madly in love with Cosette. (future perfect)

Marius will have fallen madly in love with Cosette.

__E__ 4. Ralph <u>had known</u> Mrs. Smith for years. (present perfect)

Ralph has known Mrs. Smith for years.

__B__ 5. He <u>located</u> his fishing tackle box in the garage. (past perfect)

He had located his fishing tackle box in the garage.

__C__ 6. Frank <u>will find</u> the old trunk in his aunt's attic. (simple past)

Frank found the old trunk in his aunt's attic.

__C__ 7. It <u>will take</u> a lot of time to polish the silver. (simple present)

It takes a lot of time to polish the silver.

__H__ 8. George <u>was collecting</u> for the charity. (simple past)

George collected for the charity.

__B__ 9. The letter <u>arrived</u> three days late. (future progressive)

The letter will be arriving three days late.

__E__ 10. I <u>had</u> already <u>gone</u> to that movie. (future perfect)

I will have already gone to that movie.

© Carson-Dellosa CD-3744   41

Name _____   **Verbs**

Gerunds

A **gerund** is a verb that is used as a noun. It uses the *-ing* verb ending. Like verbs, gerunds name actions or conditions. Like nouns, gerunds function as the subject, direct object, predicate nominative, or object of the preposition. A gerund can stand alone, or it can be part of a gerund phrase.

Example: Dame Van Winkle was <u>nagging</u> her husband, Rip. (verb)
           Dame Van Winkle's <u>nagging</u> made Rip's life miserable. (gerund as S)
           Rip Van Winkle hated his wife's <u>nagging</u>. (gerund as DO)
           The cause of Rip's discontent was his wife's <u>nagging</u>. (gerund as PN)
           Rip's life from the constant <u>nagging</u> was unbearable. (gerund as OP)

Underline the gerund. Choose its function in the sentence from the following: S for subject, DO for direct object, PN for predicate nominative, or OP for object of the preposition. If there is no gerund in the sentence, write NONE.

__S__ 1. <u>Studying</u> preoccupied Mary during the week of final exams.

__DO__ 2. Peter loves <u>sailing</u> on his yacht with his friends and family.

__S__ 3. <u>Smoking</u> contributed to his serious heart condition.

__S__ 4. <u>Playing</u> is the work of young children.

__PN__ 5. My favorite form of exercise is <u>jogging</u>.

__DO__ 6. Natalie enjoys <u>driving</u> her mother's four wheel drive utility vehicle.

__S__ 7. <u>Diving</u> is dangerous in this shallow lake.

__S__ 8. <u>Acting</u> is her favorite extracurricular activity.

__OP__ 9. An ineffective method of <u>studying</u> is simply memorizing.

__OP__ 10. He was preoccupied with thoughts about <u>dying</u>.

__S__ 11. <u>Whining</u> won't get you your way.

__S__ 12. <u>Stretching</u> is important after exercise.

__OP__ 13. Jasmine couldn't cope with <u>losing</u>.

__OP__ 14. Rebecca got in trouble, as usual, for <u>talking</u> with her large circle of friends.

__NONE__ 15. Daisy will be collecting food items for Thanksgiving baskets for the poor this week.

© Carson-Dellosa CD-3744   42

Name _____   **Adjectives**

Limiting and Descriptive Adjectives

An **adjective** modifies a noun (or pronoun). There are several kinds. **Descriptive adjectives** describe a noun by making the meaning more precise. There are also two kinds of **limiting adjectives** called *definite* and *indefinite* articles. The definite article *the* specifies a particular noun. The indefinite articles *a* and *an* generalize the noun.

Example: shabby couch (descriptive)
           honest priest (descriptive)
           the truth (limiting)
           a sign (limiting and used before words beginning with a consonant sound)
           an apple (limiting and used before words beginning with a vowel sound)

Underline each descriptive or limiting adjective. Classify it as descriptive (D) or limiting (L).

1. Every year many <u>curious</u>(D) visitors visit Manhattan to see what <u>the</u>(L) city is really like.

2. There are <u>good</u>(D) reasons why so many fall in love with this bustling metropolis.

3. One special moment is when <u>the</u>(L) house lights dim at the Metropolitan Opera and the sparkling chandeliers ascend into <u>the</u>(L) ceiling.

4. <u>The</u>(L) <u>golden</u>(D) statue of Prometheus in Rockefeller Center is also <u>an</u>(L) <u>enthralling</u>(D) sight.

5. <u>The</u>(L) <u>lofty</u>(D) rows of skyscrapers which make up <u>the</u>(L) <u>familiar</u>(D) skyline are another lure for the <u>first-time</u>(L) tourist.

6. Could one look up at <u>the</u>(L) Empire State Building without movie memories of <u>the</u>(L) <u>giant</u>(D) ape King Kong?

7. <u>A</u>(L) <u>leisurely</u>(D) stroll down <u>the</u>(L) <u>famous</u>(D) Mulberry Street in Little Italy will fill <u>the</u>(L) visitor's senses with <u>delectable</u>(D) sights and smells.

8. <u>The</u>(L) <u>colossal</u>(D) Statue of Liberty is <u>a</u>(L) <u>definite</u>(D) challenge to climb.

9. This <u>beautiful</u>(D) statue attracts <u>a</u>(L) <u>multitude</u> of tourists.

10. Tourists always make time to walk in that <u>incredible</u>(D) <u>green</u>(D) oasis in <u>the</u>(L) middle of Manhattan called Central Park.

© Carson-Dellosa CD-3744   43

Name _____   **Adjectives**

Comparison of Adjectives

An adjective that compares the qualities of one noun or pronoun to another (*clearer* or *more athletic*) uses the **comparative** form. An adjective that compares the qualities of more than two nouns or pronouns (*oldest* or *most dangerous*) uses the **superlative** form. Most adjectives with one syllable form their comparatives by adding *-er* and their superlative by adding *-est*. Some adjectives with two syllables only add *more* for the comparative and *most* for the superlative. Some can use either form (*more, most, -er,* or *-est*). You may need to consult the dictionary to be sure that you are using the correct form. Adjectives containing three or more syllables generally use *more* or *most*.

Example:	Adjective	Comparative form	Superlative
(1 syllable)	fast	faster	fastest
(2 syllables)	active	more active	most active
(2 syllables)	friendly	friendlier	friendliest
	friendly	more friendly	most friendly
(3 syllables)	efficient	more efficient	most efficient

Fill in the comparative and superlative forms of the adjectives listed below.

Adjective	Comparative Form	Superlative Form
1. adequate	more adequate	most adequate
2. loud	louder	loudest
3. narrow	narrower	narrowest
4. busy	busier	busiest
5. green	greener	greenest
6. cold	colder	coldest
7. sympathetic	more sympathetic	most sympathetic
8. agreeable	more agreeable	most agreeable
9. prosperous	more prosperous	most prosperous
10. selfish	more selfish	most selfish
11. greedy	greedier	greediest
12. kind	kinder	kindest
13. difficult	more difficult	most difficult
14. fantastic	more fantastic	most fantastic

© Carson-Dellosa CD-3744   44

Answer Pages

Name _____   Adjectives

Comparison of Adjectives

Fill in the blank with the correct form of the adjective.

1. (phony) The counterfeit dollar bill looked ____more phony____ than the ten dollar bill.

2. (sharp) This pencil is ____sharper____ than that one.

3. (straight) Maggie could draw the ____straightest____ lines in her class.

4. (expensive) He always buys the ____most expensive____ shoes in the store.

5. (cold) He gave me the ____coldest____ look that I ever received.

6. (convenient) This library is the ____most convenient____ one in town for the students.

7. (serious) She has always been ____more serious____ than her sister.

8. (valuable) The diamond brooch is ____more valuable____ than the ruby ring.

9. (distinguished) Meghan delivered the ____most distinguished____ speech in her grade.

10. (eager) Sally is ____more eager____ to attend the dance than Beulah.

11. (wise) The teacher's advice was ____wiser____ than the dropout's.

12. (cold) This has been the ____coldest____ winter in years.

13. (helpful) Ms. Hopkins is ____more helpful____ than Mr. Bennet.

14. (bright) Venus is the ____brightest____ star in the sky.

15. (colorful) That is the ____most colorful____ poster in the campaign.

© Carson-Dellosa CD-3744   45

Name _____   Adjectives

Pronouns as Adjectives

Pronouns take the place of nouns. Adjectives describe nouns or pronouns. The same word can function as an adjective or pronoun depending on its use in the sentence.

Example: <u>That</u> is really expensive. (pronoun)
           <u>That</u> dress is really expensive. (adjective-modifies dress)
           <u>Some</u> of you can come. (pronoun)
           <u>Some</u> students are coming with us. (adjective-modifies students)

Underline the pronoun in each sentence. Idetify the function of each as P (pronoun) or A (adjective). For this exercise, skip the limiting adjectives (articles) *a, an,* **and** *the* **when you indentify adjectives.**

- **P** 1. This is my friend, Rosilee.
- **P** 2. Bruce will buy whichever is left.
- **P** 3. Madeline can buy any car she wants.
- **P** 4. Was Bob interested in any of them?
- **P** 5. This is my friend, Albert.
- **A** 6. Betty ate some of these apples.
- **A** 7. Those girls read *Jane Eyre* in the fall.
- **A** 8. Each one found a seat.
- **P** 9. Those weren't on the shelf.
- **P** 10. Cheryl doesn't want any.
- **P** 11. Any of these are working.
- **A** 12. That responsibility is yours.

Write four of your own sentences. Use *most* **and** *these* **as both adjectives and pronouns.**

1. Those shoes are new. _____

2. Those are new. _____

3. This is the most fun I've ever had. _____

4. You have the most. _____

© Carson-Dellosa CD-3744   46

Name _____   Comparisons

Comparison of Adverbs

An **adverb** identifies the word that it modifies (verb, adjective or adverb) as having certain qualities. An adverb that compares two things uses the **comparative** form. An adverb that compares the qualities of more than two things uses the **superlative** form. Most adverbs with one syllable form their comparatives by adding *-er* and their superlatives by adding *-est*. Some adjectives with two syllables only add *more* for the comparative and *most* for the superlative. Some can use either form (*more/most* or *-er, -est*). You may need to consult the dictionary to be sure that you are using the correct form. Adverbs containing three or more syllables generally use only *more* or *most* as well as *less* or *least*.

	Example:	Positive	Comparative	Superlative
(1 syllable)		soon	sooner	soonest
(2 syllables)		often	more often	most often
(2 syllables)		friendly	friendlier	friendliest
		friendly	more friendly	most friendly
(3 syllables)		beautifully	more beautifully	most beautifully

Fill in the comparative and superlative forms.

Positive	Comparative Form	Superlative Form
1. early	earlier	earliest
2. highly	more highly	most highly
3. deep	deeper	deepest
4. bravely	more bravely	most bravely
5. gracefully	more gracefully	most gracefully
6. quickly	more quickly	most quickly
7. adequately	more adequately	most adequately
8. hard	harder	hardest
9. obviously	more obviously	most obviously
10. neatly	more neatly	most neatly
11. high	higher	highest
12. soon	sooner	soonest
13. quietly	more quietly	most quietly

© Carson-Dellosa CD-3744   47

Name _____   Comparisons

Comparison of Adverbs

Fill in the blank with the correct comparative or superlative form of the adverb.

1. (high) Lorraine can jump ____higher____ than any of the competitors.

2. (fairly) My math teacher grades ____more fairly____ than my science teacher.

3. (early) Seven o'clock in the morning is the ____earliest____ time that you can arrive at school.

4. (slowly) Randolph does his homework ____more slowly____ than Rudy.

5. (seriously) Although everyone on the bus was injured, the people in the rear were injured ____most seriously____.

6. (commonly) The ____most commonly____ found food at American barbecues is the hamburger.

7. (frequently) Trang needs to visit the dentist ____more frequently____ than she does.

8. (often) Albert jogs ____more often____ at daybreak than at sunset.

9. (thoroughly) We searched ____more thoroughly____ the second time.

10. (sensibly) Joy eats ____more sensibly____ than her brother.

11. (steadily) Blake steered the boat ____more steadily____ after the wind and rain subsided.

12. (soon) I hope that you arrive ____sooner____ than my blind date.

13. (smoothly) My new pen writes ____more smoothly____ than my old one.

14. (gracefully) Michelle danced the _____ of all the swans in *Swan Lake*. ____most gracefully____

15. (fast) Beth ran _____ of all. ____fastest____

© Carson-Dellosa CD-3744   48

Answer Pages

Comparisons

Comparison of Irregular Adjectives and Adverbs

Some commonly used adjectives and adverbs are compared irregularly.

Example:	positive	comparative	superlative
	bad (adj)	worse	worst
	badly (adv)	worse	worst

Look at the irregular comparative. Write the comparative and superlative form.

Positive	Comparative	Superlative
1. little	less	least
2. much	more	most
3. ill	worse	worst
4. many	more	most
5. well	better	best
6. far	farther	farthest
7. good	better	best

Complete each sentence using the correct comparative form of the adjective or adverb.

1. (well) I feel ____better____ than I did yesterday.

2. (many) She received the ____most____ applause at Saturday's performance.

3. (little) He received ____less____ computer training than I had.

4. (old) Aunt Marie was the ____oldest____ person at the party.

5. (badly) Malachi performed ____worst____ in the class on the pop quiz.

6. (far) Joy lives the ____farthest____ from school of all of her classmates.

Prepositions

Identifying Prepositions and Prepositional Phrases

Prepositions connect nouns and pronouns to other words in a sentence and show their relationship. They never stand alone. They introduce a prepositional phrase that contains a noun or pronoun and its modifiers. Prepositional phrases do not include verbs.

Example: She found the spoon *under* the kitchen table.
           It was the morning *before* the wedding.
           We saw a blue bird *in* the sycamore tree.

Fill in the blank with a preposition. Underline the phrase it introduces.

1. Charlotte Bronte, the author of *Jane Eyre* lived ____from____ 1816 to 1855.

2. Charlotte was the eldest ____of____ the four Bronte sisters.

3. ____During____ their childhood, Charlotte and her sister Emily attended a school that both girls hated because ____of____ its inhumane treatment ____of____ the students.

4. Charlotte wrote a scathing account ____of____ this heartless school ____in____ her book, *Jane Eyre.*

5. ____In____ 1842 Charlotte went ____to____ Brussels.

6. She worked ____for____ a while ____as____ a governess there.

7. Her heroine Jane also spent most ____of____ her time ____as____ a governess.

8. Charlotte returned home soon ____from____ Brussels.

9. She was needed desperately ____by____ her blind father, alcoholic brother, and gravely ill sisters.

10. The sisters tried publishing a book ____of____ poems, but were unsuccessful.

11. The sisters then returned ____to____ writing fiction, and each produced a novel.

12. Charlotte's first book, *The Professor*, was flatly and coldly refused ____by____ the publishers.

13. Her next novel, *Jane Eyre*, was very successful; ____from____ it she received much fame and praise.

Prepositions

Identifying Prepositions and Prepositional Phrases

Extend each sentence by adding a preposition or a prepositional phrase.

1. Meghan walked her dog ____in the park____.

2. The sparrow flew ____across the sky____.

3. The ball bounced ____into the water____.

4. His glasses fell ____off his face____.

5. Elizabeth stared ____into the distance____.

6. The loot was found ____in a cave____.

7. The house ____at the beach____ was charming.

8. The girl ____in the pink dress____ came alone.

9. Irene baked cookies ____in a brick oven____.

10. A chattering squirrel ran ____into the tree____.

11. The barge plowed ____up the river____.

12. Carla won a trip ____to Mississippi____.

13. The Green family lives ____around the corner____.

14. We were hungry ____on the day____ that we prepared the feast.

15. The bouquet ____of flowers____ was a thoughtful gift.

16. The map ____in the atlas____ was not up-to-date.

17. The face ____in the photo____ looked tired.

18. The roses ____from the garden____ were stunning in full bloom.

19. The boys came ____inside the house____ when it started raining.

20. Our parade will begin ____in an hour____.

Prepositions

Identifying Prepositions and Prepositional Phrases

Fill in the blank with a preposition. Underline the phrase it introduces.

1. Mr. Post is riding the Orient Express ____from____ Paris ____to____ Venice.

2. Bob was ____at____ the movie theater when the fire started.

3. The capital ____of____ Maine is Augusta.

4. That cantankerous black cat lives ____on____ this street.

5. The remote was hidden ____under____ the sofa cushion.

6. The makeup artist turned the actor ____into____ a monster.

7. We left the disappointing performance ____after____ the intermission.

8. A crowd gathered ____at____ the scene ____of____ the accident.

9. Ralph has been anxiously waiting all week ____for____ that letter.

10. The painting fell ____off____ the wall ____for____ no apparent reason.

11. The content kitten slept ____beside____ its mother.

12. The fireworks will begin ____after____ dark.

13. The invitation went ____to____ the wrong address.

14. The ball rolled ____into____ the bushes.

15. She climbed ____up____ the steep stone stairs ____in____ the castle.

16. The dog waited ____beside____ his master ____until____ dusk every evening.

17. A really pretty girl sat ____beside____ Andy ____at____ the movies.

18. The boy ____in____ my class won the election.

19. Sylvia and her mother set flowers ____on____ the new dining room table.

20. ____after____ the storm, we picked up branches and raked fallen leaves.

Answer Pages

Name _____   Conjunctions

Coordinating Conjunctions

Conjunctions join words or groups of words. One kind of conjunction is the **coordinating conjunction**. Coordinating conjunctions connect single words, phrases (combinations of words that go together within sentences) and clauses (word combinations containing a subject and predicate) that are of the same importance or rank. The most common ones are *and*, *but*, and *or*.

Example: The children feasted on cookies *and* milk. (joins words)
The kids asked me to come *and* join them. (joins phrases)
I can go, *but* you can't. (joins clauses or simple sentences)

Read each sentence. Supply an appropriate coordinating conjunction. Write on the line if it joins words (W), phrases (P), or clauses/simple sentences (C).

_C_ 1. Roses need good drainage, ____but____ their leaves will turn yellow.

_W_ 2. Eugene considered the punishment cruel ____and____ unusual.

_P_ 3. It is possible ____but____ not very likely.

_C_ 4. We waited in the terminal for hours, ____but____ our connection didn't ever arrive.

_P_ 5. He was born and raised in Ohio, ____and____ now lives in New York.

_C_ 6. Sue decides on the itinerary, ____and____ Joe makes the travel arrangements.

_P_ 7. Sam has been driving ____and____ making sales calls for weeks.

_C_ 8. I couldn't go, ____but____ Janet could.

_W_ 9. He gladly received her hugs ____and____ kisses.

_W_ 10. Carmen ____and____ Mimi won't admit their ages.

_W_ 11. Marcus ____and____ Rudolpho won't admit their weights.

_W_ 12. I don't eat fat ____or____ sugar.

_C_ 13. Alexander looked everywhere, ____but____ the book had vanished.

_W_ 14. The homeless shelter needs donations of food ____and____ clothing.

© Carson-Dellosa CD-3744   53

Name _____   Conjunctions

Correlative Conjunctions

Conjunctions join words or groups of words. **Correlative conjunctions** are paired connective words that link single words, phrases (combinations of words that go together within sentences), and clauses (word combinations containing subjects and predicates). The correlative conjunctions are: *both .... and; neither . .. nor; whether .... or; either .... or; not only .. . but* (or *but also*).

Examples: She has met *neither* Polly *nor* Renee. (joins words)
She can prepare *either* a detailed outline *or* a structured overview. (joins phrases)
I don't know *whether* Peter will go *or* Jack will. (joins clauses)

Read each sentence and supply the appropriate correlative conjunctions in the blanks. Write in the blank if the correlative conjunctions join words (W), phrases (P) or clauses (C).

_W_ 1. You will need ____neither____ pencil ____nor____ paper.

_W_ 2. The toddler drinks ____either____ milk ____or____ apple juice.

_P_ 3. Blake's exercise program includes ____not only____ aerobic workouts ____but also____ weight training.

_W_ 4. ____Either____ cookies ____or____ potato chips should appear so regularly in your lunch box.

_W_ 5. He is guilty of ____both____ pickpocketing ____and____ burglary.

_P_ 6. ____Not only____ did he take my wallet ____but also____ my television.

_P_ 7. You must decide ____whether____ to ask Anne ____or____ Maria.

_C_ 8. ____Either____ help me ____or____ leave me alone.

_W_ 9. ____Both____ Jim ____and____ Brian asked Krystal to dance.

_P_ 10. I can't decide ____whether____ I want to see a movie, ____neither____ or eat dinner.

_W_ 11. The menu includes ____both____ Cajun ____and____ French food.

_C_ 12. ____Either____ come with me, ____or____ I'll go alone.

© Carson-Dellosa CD-3744   54

Name _____   Conjunctions

Subordinating Conjunctions

Subordinating conjunctions connect clauses and indicate that one of the two clauses is more important to the basic meaning of the sentence. The less important (dependent) clause is introduced by the subordinating conjunction and gives additional meaning to the main clause. There are many subordinating conjunctions. Some of the most common include *after, although, as, because, before, if, since, unless, whatever, when, whenever, where, wherever,* and *while.* Subordinating conjunctions can appear in the beginning or in the middle of a sentence.

Example: **Until** you finish your homework, don't turn on the television.
Barbara will decorate for the party **while** I wrap the presents.

Circle the subordinating conjunction. Underline the dependent clause that it introduces.

1. (If) you are a serious traveler, you should carry the right gear.

2. Use an all-purpose, water resistant camera with a zoom lens (when) you take pictures.

3. (Although) you may not know the uses for all of its 31 tools, bring along a Swiss army knife.

4. (If) your dog must come, bring a collapsible dog bowl with a waterproof, nylon lining.

5. Carry a fold-up bag inside your luggage (when) you plan to bring home a lot of souvenirs.

6. (Unless) you know that the weather will be consistently cold, carry a convertible jacket with removable sleeves.

7. There are also cotton pants with zip-off legs (if) you find yourself warm enough to be in shorts.

8. (Since) health and safety are always considerations, carry an emergency first aid kit.

9. (If) you are concerned about foreign fire safety codes, bring along your own lightweight, battery-powered smoke alarm.

10. (Because) you do not always find your bare feet in the most sanitary of places, carry skid-resistant rubber shoes with mesh netting uppers.

© Carson-Dellosa CD-3744   55

Name _____   Interjections

Using Interjections

Interjections express some emotion and have no grammatical connection to the sentence. They can be followed by a comma or an exclamation point. Some commonly used interjections include: *Oh, Great, Wow, Ouch, Hey, Please,* and *No.*

Example: *Oh,* so there you are!
Great! I left my umbrella at home.

Add an interjection to each sentence.

1. ____Please____ ! Do not interrupt the speaker.

2. ____Wow____ , what a wonderful time we had on safari!

3. ____Wow____ , this is a fabulous pasta primavera.

4. ____Oh____ , what a fabulous experience for the students!

5. ____Great____ ! So you have finally decided to go.

6. ____Hey____ , what an incredibly rude thing to say!

7. ____No____ , I can't take it anymore.

8. ____Hey____ , you look great in those high heels!

9. ____Great____ ! The police are coming.

10. ____Oh____ , the earth is shaking!

11. ____No____ , get out of here!

12. ____Wow____ , I love this class!

13. ____Please____ ! Stop blaring that radio.

14. ____Ouch____ ! Come help me.

15. ____Hey____ , I need more time!

© Carson-Dellosa CD-3744   56

Answer Pages

Parts of Speech Review

Identify the part of speech of each underlined word in the paragraphs that follow. Write the part of speech on the numbered line. Use the following abbreviations:

noun (N)	adjective (ADJ)	pronoun (P)	conjunction (C)
verb (V)	adverb (ADV)	preposition (PREP)	interjection (IN)

Mont-St-Michel

Mont-St-Michel dominates the white beaches between the provinces of Normandy and
                                 1   2

Brittany in France. If you have the opportunity to view Mont-St-Michel as it emerges from
                         3   4

the ocean at high tide, you will agree that it is a truly unforgettable experience. It is such
                   5   6

an architectural wonder that it has often been called "Marvel of the West."
     7

The legend says that in the eighth century, Archangel St. Michael appeared to a local
                         8   9

bishop and ordered him to build a chapel on top of a 258 foot high mount. An abbey
            10   11

quickly followed, which in order to accommodate the increasing number of pilgrims from
               12   13

all over Europe, was constantly embellished and enlarged with new constructions, some
                                  14

times built on top of each other.
                     15

The result of all this construction is one of medieval Europe's masterpieces. Indeed, it
      16   17   18

is surely one of the world's great masterpieces.
   19   20

1. PREP	6. ADV	11. N	16. N
2. N	7. ADJ	12. P	17. ADJ
3. V	8. ADJ	13. PREP	18. IN
4. P	9. ADJ	14. C	19. ADV
5. V	10. P	15. P	20. ADJ

57

Parts of Speech Review

Identify the part of speech of each underlined word in the paragraphs that follow. Write the part of speech on the numbered line. Use the following abbreviations:

noun (N)	adjective (ADJ)	pronoun (P)	conjunction (C)
verb (V)	adverb (ADV)	preposition (PREP)	interjection (IN)

Demeter and Persephone

The story of Demeter and Persephone was first told by Homer in a Greek poem dating
back to the seventh century. It tells the tragic tale of Demeter, the goddess of the harvest,
and her daughter, Persephone.

One day Persephone was on Earth picking flowers. Suddenly the ground opened up
and she was taken hostage by Hades, the lord of the underworld.

Demeter could not get over her grief. The year was dreadful for mankind all over the
Earth because Demeter allowed nothing to grow. When it became apparent that all
mankind would die of famine, Zeus, the king of the gods, decided to intervene.

Zeus sent his messenger Hermes down to the kingdom of the dead to secure the
release of Persephone. Hades reluctantly agreed to release her only if she would return
to him for four months every year. This length of time was decided upon because she
had eaten four pomegranate seeds while in captivity, and this act bound her to Hades for
eternity.

Demeter was overjoyed to see her daughter. The Earth became fertile again. But
every year when Persephone returned to her husband Hades, Demeter turned the earth
cold and barren once more.

1. ADV	6. N	11. V	16. N
2. V	7. PREP	12. N	17. ADV
3. PREP	8. ADV	13. V	18. P
4. N	9. N	14. V	19. ADJ
5. N	10. C	15. P	20. ADV

58

Simple Subject and Simple Predicate

In order to be a sentence (or complete thought), two elements are necessary: a **subject** (the person, place, or thing spoken about) and a **predicate** (says something about the person, place or thing). The **simple subject** (SS) is the key word that the sentence is about. The **simple predicate** (SP) is the verb (action or linking) that describes the action of the subject or some condition about the subject. Modifiers (including adjectives, adverbs, and prepositional phrases) are not included in the simple subject or simple predicate.

Example:
- key words only:
Roger / returned.
  SS   SP
- with modifiers:
Jubilant Roger / returned in triumph.
        SS   SP
- with modifiers and an object of the action verb:
Jubilant Roger / quickly returned the stolen masterpiece to the museum.
        SS   SP
- with modifiers and a condition about the subject following the linking verb:
Roger / was jubilant about the recovery of the masterpiece.
  SS   SP

Underline the simple subject. Circle the simple predicate.

1. A great way to get to Vancouver, British Columbia, is by train.
2. The train rumbles though spectacular transcontinental scenery.
3. Riders cross the Rockies, the Canadian prairies, and the lake-strewn Canadian Shield.
4. Train passengers see almost nothing of the cities and towns on the way.
5. Instead they see hazy rivers, ridges thick with evergreens, and assorted, pastoral landscapes.
6. The Canadian Rockies route through Banff and Lake Louise is probably the most striking.
7. Spiral tunnels twist and climb through the mountains.
8. Soon Calgary comes into view.
9. It is followed by two days of nothing but prairie.
10. The Canadian Shield follows the prairie with its hundreds of miles of rock, birch, aspen, and lakes.

59

Simple Subject and Simple Predicate

Add the sentence part (subject or predicate) that is missing. Underline the simple subject and circle the simple predicate.

1. The gloomy weather _____ lasted all day _____.
2. _____ The cool water _____ felt good on his parched tongue.
3. The long canoe ride _____ wore me out _____.
4. The cuckoo clock _____ annoyed me _____.
5. _____ My friends and I _____ sat on a bench in the school yard.
6. _____ Marie _____ burst into laughter at the sight.
7. The stuffed picnic basket _____ toppled over _____.
8. _____ The school funds _____ will be used for improvements to the school library.
9. Her gigantic purse _____ fell on the floor _____.
10. The sensitive artist _____ cried at the opening _____.
11. _____ Our family reunion _____ will be held in the middle of July.
12. The reason for the error _____ made me angry _____.
13. _____ The car seat _____ felt very hot to the touch.
14. The torn photograph _____ is my favorite _____.
15. The aerobic workout _____ was too difficult _____.
16. _____ My book _____ was found behind the gym.
17. The memory in his computer _____ was not enough _____.
18. The veal stew _____ simmered all day _____.
19. _____ That word _____ could be found in the dictionary.
20. _____ Peter _____ wanted to carry the flag.

60

Answer Pages

Name _____ Sentence Parts

Compound Subjects

The **subject** answers the question "Who?" or "What?" In some sentences there are two or more nouns that serve as the subject of the same verb.

Example: Mabel and Ben wrote their book reports together.
The tall girl and the freckle-faced boy were finalists in the essay contest.

Underline the nouns for each compound subject.

1. The computer and the printer were ruined in the flood.

2. The white roses, red and yellow columbine, and the lacy fern made a pretty bouquet.

3. Five pens, two three-pocket notebooks, and one pair of scissors were on her school supply list.

4. Oregano, parsley, and rosemary are easy herbs to grow in your garden.

5. Zucchini and asparagus are Manuel's favorite vegetables.

6. Melissa and Shelley disliked the movie enough to leave in the middle.

7. The Negro Speaks of Rivers and Mother to Son are great poems by Langston Hughes.

8. The dinghy and the sailboat belong to my uncle.

9. The heavy traffic and the summer heat made Allen tense and uncomfortable.

10. The landscape and the portrait will be hung in the parlor.

11. More memory and a larger monitor are needed to upgrade my computer.

12. My collie and the cat next door are great friends.

13. Samuel and his sister are often late for school.

14. The script and the schedule were not in Lyla's briefcase.

15. Mrs. Finley and her black poodle are often seen at local dog shows.

© Carson-Dellosa CD-3744   61

Name _____ Sentence Parts

Compound Predicate

A sentence has a **compound predicate** if there are two or more verbs that each have the same subject.

Example: We ate and drank until we were full.
(The subject of both verbs is We)
The watch and the ring cost a lot, but were worth the money.
(The subject of both verbs is watch and ring)

Underline the verbs. Write S on the line if it is a simple sentence (the verbs have the same subject).

_____ 1. She led and we followed.

__S__ 2. The spoiled child cried and cried for more candy.

__S__ 3. The photographer framed and shot a perfect picture.

__S__ 4. Sal will wash and dry the dishes.

_____ 5. We heard a crash, and a scream followed.

_____ 6. The rain poured and the wind roared.

__S__ 7. Faith danced and sang to the music.

__S__ 8. Melissa and Bert found the purse and returned it.

__S__ 9. The large dog slobbered and jumped all over me.

_____ 10. We prune and water the garden twice a week.

_____ 11. Patrick mopped and swept the floor.

__S__ 12. John and his sister hurried to the counter and bought two tickets.

__S__ 13. Patty washed and dried her pretty auburn hair.

__S__ 14. Don't slip and slide on the wet floor.

__S__ 15. I tried studying but fell asleep.

© Carson-Dellosa CD-3744   62

Name _____ Sentence Parts

Compound Predicate

Rewrite each simple sentence with a compound predicate. Remember that both verbs must accompany the same subject for the sentence to be simple.

Example: We sat on the sofa.   We sat and talked on the sofa.
I felt sorry for her.   I felt sorry for her and forgave her.

1. The children played in the park.

   The children laughed and played in the park.

2. The brothers were arguing in view of everyone.

   The brothers were fighting and arguing in view of everyone.

3. The driver grew sleepy.

   The driver grew sleepy and pulled over to rest.

4. The class painted with watercolors.

   The class painted with water colors and then went out to play.

5. The girls watched videos at the slumber party.

   The girls watched videos and ate popcorn at the slumber party.

6. The talented girl could sing beautifully.

   The talented girl could sing and dance beautifully.

7. The fire started in the attic.

   The fire started and ended in the attic.

8. Sam found a wallet on the ground.

   Sam found a wallet on the ground and turned it in.

9. The large dog slobbered all over me.

   The large dog jumped and slobbered all over me.

10. Ellen closed the door after Bob left.

    Ellen closed the door and cried after Bob left.

© Carson-Dellosa CD-3744   63

Name _____ Sentence Parts

The Complete Subject and Predicate

The **complete subject** contains the simple subject and any additional words that tell you who or what the sentence is speaking about. The **complete predicate** contains the simple predicate plus all other words that talk about the actions of the subject or condition of the subject following a linking verb.

Example: The jolly young man / told good jokes all the time.
complete subject   complete predicate (with action verb)
The jolly young man / is a great joke teller.
complete subject   complete predicate (with linking verb)

Underline the complete subject in each sentence once. Underline the complete predicate twice.

1. The celebrated writer Mark Twain was actually a man named Samuel L. Clemens.

2. As a young man, Samuel worked on the riverboats that travelled up and down the Mississippi.

3. The name, Mark Twain, was adapted from a riverboat term.

4. Mark Twain means "two fathoms" deep.

5. His admiring readers think that his writing is much deeper than a mere two fathoms.

6. His first major work was published in 1867.

7. It was a humorous sketch called The Celebrated Jumping Frog of Calaveras County.

8. Two years later he wrote the critically acclaimed Innocents Abroad.

9. His reputation grew around the world.

10. For the next forty years he wrote some of America's most acclaimed literature.

11. This included essays, autobiographies, travel sketches, novels and short stories.

12. He perfected the use of American Western dialect in his stories.

13. His writings, although sometimes controversial for their treatment of racial issues, remain fresh and alive today.

14. One of his best-loved works, The Adventures of Huckleberry Finn, still flames the imaginations of young people everywhere.

© Carson-Dellosa CD-3744   64

Answer Pages

© Carson-Dellosa CD-3744   115

Answer Pages

Independent and Dependent Clauses

An **independent (main) clause** can stand alone as a sentence. A **dependent (subordinate) clause** contains a subject and verb, but it does not express a complete thought and can't stand alone as a sentence. The dependent clause must be attached to the independent clause to complete the meaning. Dependent clauses often begin with a subordinating conjunction such as *although, because, if, since, until,* and *when.* They may also begin with relative pronouns such as *who, which,* or *that.*

Example: *Separately:*
Michael bought the painting at an auction. (independent)
which was a Van Gogh (dependent)
After participating in a bidding war (dependent)
Combined to make a sentence:
After participating in a bidding war, Michael bought the painting, which was a Van Gogh, at an auction.
(combination of two dependent and one independent clause)

Identify each clause as independent (IN) or dependent (D). Underline the subordinating conjunction or relative pronoun if there is one. No punctuation or capitalization is provided.

D   1. until you understand
D   2. since I have cleaned my room
IN   3. she finished her homework
D   4. before he became an archaeologist
IN   5. We saw an elephant
D   6. who buy their tickets in advance
IN   7. Jean makes the best candy
D   8. after the music stopped
IN   9. the microwave is broken
D   10. which is broken again
IN   11. Beth wears sensible walking shoes
D   12. since the walk is long

© Carson-Dellosa CD-3744   69

Independent and Dependent Clauses

Identify each clause as independent (IN) or dependent (D). Underline the subordinating conjunction or relative pronoun if there is one. No punctuation or capitalization is provided.

IN   1. she wears too much makeup
D   2. since she is under a lot of stress
D   3. until the entire project is complete
IN   4. we were thirty minutes late for the appointment
D   5. because you're afraid
IN   6. they felt more comfortable with me
D   7. if the turkey is not refrigerated
D   8. although the report was in plan view
D   9. which is in demand
D   10. that I know
IN   11. shadows are longer in the winter
IN   12. it is homemade
D   13. when the plant is over watered
IN   14. it was raining
D   15. because good records were not kept
D   16. until the light bulb was invented
D   17. that I wear to church
IN   18. Sal is arachnophobic
D   19. before it can be eaten
IN   20. you are strange

© Carson-Dellosa CD-3744   70

Dependent Clauses and Other Fragments

A sentence is a complete thought containing a subject and verb. A **dependent clause** is an incomplete thought that has a subject and verb. Other kinds of incomplete sentences are called **fragments.**

Example: She told me. (sentence)
while I wait (dependent clause)
running through the crowd (fragment)

Define each group of words as a sentence (S), dependent clause (D), or fragment (F). No punctuation or capitalization is provided.

S   1. listen to me
F   2. to listen to them
D   3. when I listen to them
S   4. Matt sat next to me
D   5. who sat next to me
F   6. next to me
F   7. when stating his opinion
D   8. when he stated his opinion
S   9. he stated his opinion
S   10. I protested the new rule
D   11. until I protested
F   12. protesting the new rule
S   13. please repeat the question
F   14. repeating the question
D   15. who repeated the question
S   16. Meg defined the word

F   17. to define the word
D   18. which defines the word
D   19. before you go
S   20. you go
D   21. before going
D   22. who lives in a castle
F   23. like living in a castle
D   24. who lives in a castle
S   25. try to win
F   26. trying to win
D   27. unless you try to win
F   28. streaking through the sky
S   29. it streaked through the sky
D   30. while it was streaking
S   31. the alarm rang
F   32. hearing the alarm

© Carson-Dellosa CD-3744   71

Making Fragments into Sentences

Rewrite each fragment below, making it into a complete sentence.

1. by reserving a ticket By reserving a ticket, you are sure to have a place to sit.

2. watching an old sitcom on television I was only watching an old sitcom on television.

3. to live in the country He would love to live in the country.

4. twirling ballerinas on the dance floor Michael is good at twirling ballerinas on the dance floor.

5. for conserving energy Thank you for conserving energy.

6. having lost his way Ignatius was afraid of having lost his way.

7. through the garden and across the pond Please go through the garden and across the pond.

8. to escape from the wicked warlock They ran quickly to escape from the wicked warlock.

9. from the looks of those shoes From the looks of those shoes, you need a new pair.

10. squeezing through a crack in the fence I saw the cat squeezing through a crack in the fence.

© Carson-Dellosa CD-3744   72

Answer Pages

Name _____   Sentence Structure

Complex Sentences

A **complex sentence** contains one independent clause and one or more dependent clauses. The independent clause is the more important of the two, and the dependent clause modifies it in some way. A dependent clause can appear inside the independent clause as well as before it or after it. It is usually introduced by a subordinating conjunction or a relative pronoun.

Example: When we heard how much the repairs would cost, we decided to buy a new car.
   We didn't think that we could afford a new car, until we saw the cost of repairs.
   The girl who is driving the red convertible is my sister.

Write CX if the sentence is complex. Underline the independent clause once. Underline the dependent clause(s) twice.

CX 1. If you plan the party, I will come.

_____ 2. I will take the early flight if absolutely necessary.

_____ 3. Because of her great personality, Lauren is very popular.

CX 4. Mr. West, a computer programmer, will help us set up our new computer.

CX 5. The new teacher who is being evaluated is in Room 306.

CX 6. When the summer gets hot, Alice longs for snowy mountains.

CX 7. Since the party is on a school night, I can't go.

CX 8. The dog that looks like a stray belongs to my neighbor.

CX 9. The state which is my favorite is Maine.

CX 10. Rebecca is my friend who loves animals.

CX 11. You must put on your seatbelt before I start the car.

CX 12. Whenever we want great homemade pie, we go to my grandmother's house.

CX 13. Because you are my friend, I will tell you my secret!

_____ 14. The girl wearing the yellow headband is my sister.

CX 15. Mrs. Scott, who was my third grade teacher, is my new neighbor.

73

Name _____   Sentence Structure

Complex Sentences

Underline the dependent clause in each complex sentence. Do nothing to the sentence if it is not complex.

1. My sister, who spends most of her time at the library, is an avid reader of nonfiction in the area of environmental concerns.

2. Until you clean your room and wash the dog, don't expect to get your weekly allowance.

3. The Mexican tour operator in Cancun specializes in tours that introduce foreign visitors to local Mayan Indians.

4. Alex is a friendly and energetic person who loves to be in the middle of active group projects.

5. If each class contributes a Thanksgiving basket with all the trimmings, our school will be able to help forty needy families.

6. The science fiction writer Isaac Asimov is able to create a whole new world that is completely foreign to us.

7. In Malaysia we saw a temple with a reclining Buddha and big dragons out front which made for a good photo opportunity.

8. Since I didn't give the elephant the bananas fast enough, she gave me a special spray of water with her trunk.

9. It is easy to catch a taxi in New York, although the drivers often don't speak much English.

10. If you enjoy visiting old southern plantations, try Nottaway Plantation in Donaldsonville, Louisiana.

11. Alice Walker, who is best known for her novels, has also written several books of poetry.

12. Ralph, who is rarely at home, has an active social life.

13. Although the necklace was very inexpensive, Cheryl cherished it for sentimental reasons.

14. Until night fell, my whole family worked tirelessly in our newly-planted vegetable garden.

15. By the time she was twenty, Kendall had finished her bachelor's degree in Anthropology.

74

Name _____   Sentence Structure

Complex Sentence Review

Classify each of the following sentences as follows:
   (S)Simple   (C)Compound   (CX)Complex.

CX 1. If you need any help, I'm available.

CX 2. You won't believe what I found out.

C 3. Mrs. Meyers wants to go to New Zealand, but her husband would prefer to go to Kenya.

S 4. Peggy isn't paying attention in class today.

C 5. Clarissa and I have been best friends since fifth grade, and we probably always will be best friends.

CX 6. I think that the artist who does the best portraits is this one.

C 7. We spent two hours on the tour bus, and then we began a walking tour of London.

CX 8. Betty would be a good writer if she would only be more conscientious about revising.

S 9. I actually witnessed the shoplifter take an expensive watch and slip it in his pocket.

CX 10. I know him because we went to the same summer camp last year.

CX 11. I was confused about the time until I noticed that the electricity had gone out.

C 12. I want you to come, but it is your decision.

C 13. Drew's birthday is on Thursday, and I can't think of a really good present for him.

CX 14. Meghan has a schedule conflict this weekend that she doesn't know how to resolve.

S 15. Patricia looked stunning in the blue suit.

C 16. Sam has several inventions patented, and he is hard at work on another one.

S 17. Alyssa has been enjoying books from a very early age.

S 18. My cat awakens me a dawn every morning.

CX 19. After he gets a good bath, my dog can't wait to roll in the dirt.

S 20. Will you be responsible for collecting the money?

75

Name _____   Sentence Structure

Complex Sentence Review

Classify each of the following sentences as follows:
   (S)Simple   (C)Compound   (CX)Complex

C 1. Father put the baby to bed at seven o'clock, but she didn't fall asleep for a long time.

S 2. William Shakespeare wrote plays and poetry.

CX 3. After I finish practicing piano, I'll help you make the fudge.

S 4. We heard the siren and saw the police car.

S 5. Meghan couldn't wake up this morning.

CX 6. When Germaine saw Keisha, it was love at first sight.

C 7. Carla would prefer to vacation in the Caribbean, but I'd rather spend time in Europe.

S 8. Many of Jane Austen's novels have been made into successful movies over the past forty years.

CX 9. Because she couldn't swim a stroke, Vicki didn't enjoy boating or any water-related recreation.

S 10. The flimsy cover of the dictionary fell off from constant use.

CX 11. I need to shorten the hem of this dress and add new buttons if I'm going to wear it for another season.

C 12. Beth takes French and Bob takes Spanish.

S 13. A live performance of *The Nutcracker* or *Swan Lake* is always a treat for ballet lovers.

CX 14. Carl felt much better when his diet improved.

CX 15. After we decorated the Christmas tree, we stood back and admired our work.

C 16. The school play is this weekend, but I won't be able to attend.

S 17. Our sofa converts into a double bed.

C 18. Are you fond of winter, or do you prefer the summer?

CX 19. When Jasmine can't sleep, she drinks warm milk.

S 20. Are you just arriving or just leaving?

76

Answer Pages

Name _____ Sentence Structure

Complex Sentence Review

Classify each of the following sentences as follows:

(S)Simple (C)Compound (CX)Complex

(1) The islands of Hawaii are a world of their own. (2) Each has a distinct flavor, yet all share in the heavenly beauty of the tropics. (3) The most likely spot to begin exploring is Honolulu, Oahu which is the island with famous Waikiki Beach. (4) One special sight here is the natural puka in the rugged coastline known as the Blow Hole. (5) A geyser effect is created by the action of the waves being forced through the lava tube. (6) Also to be found in Oahu is the Iolani Palace, the only house of royalty on American soil. (7) Finally, on this island few visitors miss the opportunity to see USS Arizona Battleship Memorial in Pearl Harbor.

(8) Maui, the second largest island, is considered by many to be the most beautiful. (9) It contains the world's largest dormant volcano, and it is known for its spectacular sunsets and great beaches. (10) Another famous sight to view is the Iao Needle, a 1,200-foot green monolith, which rises hauntingly from the valley floor. (11) The old whaling seaport of Lahaina with its quaint streets and shops is another Maui treasure. (12) From the eastern shore at Hana, the ocean stretches seemingly forever, and it is alive with coral and exotically colored fish.

(13) The Big Island, Hawaii, is the youngest and southernmost in the chain. (14) It contains Volcanoes National Park which was established to preserve the mysteriously beautiful landscape of Mauna Loa volcano and its active neighbor Kilaueau. (15) Kilaueau erupts regularly and in spectacular style with steaming fire pits and giant lava tubes. (16) A popular activity is flightseeing over the volcanoes from a helicopter.

(17) Another unique island is Kauai with its famous Fern Grotto which is a secluded cave framed by gigantic fishtail ferns. (18) A not-to-be-missed sight is the Waimea Canyon, often called the "Grand Canyon of the Pacific." (19) Here you will see green jungles, and breathtaking waterfalls, cliffs and canyons. (20) Hawaii has something for everyone, and, therefore, it is one of the world's favorite destinations for tourists.

1. S   6. S   11. S   16. S
2. C   7. S   12. C   17. CX
3. CX 8. S   13. S   18. S
4. S   9. C   14. CX 19. S
5. S   10. CX 15. S   20. C

77

Name _____ Sentence Structure

Sentence Expanding with When, Where, and How

Read the core sentence. Expand it to include information about *when*, *where*, or *how* it happened.

Example: Chad worked on his research project.
tirelessly (how)
at the library (where)
everyday after school (when)
Chad worked tirelessly on his research project at the library everyday after school.

1. **Mario found the path.**
   Mario found the path while jogging.

2. **The rain poured.**
   The rain poured all night long.

3. **We descended the mountain trail.**
   We descended the mountain trail very carefully.

4. **Beth concocted an original dessert.**
   Last night, Beth concocted an original dessert.

5. **Evelyn planned her spring garden.**
   Evelyn planned her spring garden with great enthusiasm.

6. **Senator Blair continued campaigning.**
   Senator Blair continued campaigning late into the evening.

78

Name _____ Sentence Structure

Sentence Combining

Read the two sentences. Underline the part in the second sentence which can be used to expand the first sentence. Rewrite the first sentence to include the underlined information. No changes in words or punctuation are necessary.

Example: The children should not see that film.
The children are below thirteen years of age.
The children below thirteen years of age should not see that film.

1. The candidates will speak at the university.
   The candidates are running for governor.

   The candidates running for governor will speak at the university.

2. The road construction is to be completed by next June.
   The road construction is causing heavy traffic at this time.

   The road construction causing heavy traffic at this time is to be completed by next June.

3. These students are taking advanced placement courses.
   These students are in their senior year.

   These students in their senior year are taking advanced placement courses.

4. The fund raiser should produce considerable revenue.
   The fund raiser is scheduled for next month.

   The fund raiser scheduled for next month should produce considerable revenue.

5. The neighborhood filed a grievance.
   The neighborhood is receiving assistance from the Environmental Protection Agency.

   The neighborhood receiving assistance from the Environmental Protection Agency filed a grievance.

79

Name _____ Word Usage

Pronouns after *Than* and *As*

When a sentence compares one person to another using **than** or **as**, the pronoun used after than or as may be either in the nominative case (*I, you, he, she, we, they*) or the objective case (*me, you, him, her,* or *them*). To determine which case is correct, expand the sentence.

Example: Mike is shorter than I. (nominative case needed)
Mike is shorter than I am.
Jane is not as talented as she. (nominative case needed)
Jane is not as talented as she is.
Cliff likes Alice more than me. (objective case needed)
Cliff likes Alice better than he likes me.
Brad likes Alice more than I. (nominative case needed)
Brad likes Alice more than I like Alice.

Circle the pronoun in the correct case. Write the expanded sentence. If there are two possible expanded sentences, circle both pronouns and write both expanded sentences.

1. Luciano sings as well as (I, me).
   Luciano sings as well as I sing.

2. Manuel is not as well known as (he, him).
   Manuel is not as well known as he is.

3. Gigi knows him better than (I, me).
   Gigi knows him better than I know him.
   Gigi knows him better than he knows me.

4. Roger delivered a better speech than (she, her).
   Roger delivered a better speech than she delivered.

5. Jeff loves Becky more than (I, me).
   Jeff loves Becky more than I do.
   Jeff loves Becky more than he loves me.

6. Jack can run faster than (he, him).
   Jack can run faster than he can run.

80

Answer Pages

Name _____ Word Usage

Who, Whom, Whoever, and Whomever

Who and **whoever** are used as subjects of verbs (nominatives). **Whom** and **whomever** are used as direct objects (objects of verbs) or objects of prepositions.

> Example: Jack is the one <u>who</u> got caught. (*who* is the subject of *got*)
> <u>Whoever</u> owns this credit card must first show identification.
> (*whoever* is the subject of the verb *owns*)
> Give this to <u>whomever</u> you want. (*whomever* is object of the preposition *to*)
> That is the woman whom I saw on the train.
> (*whom* is direct object of the verb *saw*)

Fill in the blank with the correct pronoun—*who, whoever, whom,* or *whomever.*

1. Jack asked Jill _____**whom**_____ she invited to the dance.
2. With everyone in costume, I don't know _____**who**_____ is who.
3. Vote for _____**whoever**_____ you want.
4. This is a lady _____**who**_____ is worthy of your trust.
5. I know _____**whom**_____ it was that cheated.
6. Miss Scarlet is the guest _____**who**_____ committed murder.
7. _____**Who**_____ is responsible for this mess?
8. Mr. Washington is the man _____**who**_____ we met.
9. Can you guess _____**whom**_____ we saw at the mall?
10. The mysterious woman _____**who**_____ was here left you a message.
11. Please ask _____**whomever**_____ is nearby to come and help.
12. The person to _____**whom**_____ I gave the money has vanished.

© Carson-Dellosa CD-3744   81

Name _____

Who's & Whose

Who's is a contraction for "Who is". **Whose** can be an interrogative pronoun that indicates possession or a relative pronoun (introducing a clause) in the possessive case.

> Example: <u>Who's</u> coming? (contraction for "Who is")
> <u>Whose</u> recipe is this? (interrogative pronoun showing possession)
> The man <u>whose</u> recipe won first place is from Louisiana.
> (relative pronoun showing possession)

Fill in the blank with Who's or Whose. Decide how the word is used and label it as a contraction (C), interrogative (INT), or relative pronoun (RP).

_I_ 1. _____**Whose**_____ name did you pick?
_C_ 2. _____**Who's**_____ your first choice for class president?
_RP_ 3. I know _____**whose**_____ name you picked.
_C_ 4. _____**Who's**_____ going to pick up the children after school?
_I_ 5. _____**Whose**_____ mother is carpooling today?
_RP_ 6. That is the girl _____**whose**_____ mother is driving today.
_I_ 7. _____**Whose**_____ signature is this?
_C_ 8. _____**Who's**_____ the most likely one to get caught?
_RP_ 9. The student _____**whose**_____ report card had all A's was the envy of everyone.
_I_ 10. _____**Whose**_____ ten dollar bill is this on the ground?
_C_ 11. _____**Who's**_____ the owner of this ten dollar bill?
_RP_ 12. The woman _____**whose**_____ picture hangs in the office is a former principal.

© Carson-Dellosa CD-3744   82

Name _____ Word Usage

Their, There and They're

Their is a pronominal adjective that is the possessive form of "they." **There** is an adverb meaning "at that place or at that point." **They're** is a pronoun and verb contracted from "they are."

> Example: Do you know their address? (the address belongs to them)
> <u>There</u> is the bibliography. (at that place)
> <u>They're</u> merely acquaintances. (contraction of "they are")

Write either *their, there* or *they're* in the blanks below.

1. _____**There**_____ won't be time for a thorough review of the material.
2. I don't want to ruin _____**their**_____ plans.
3. Do you know _____**their**_____ motivation?
4. _____**They're**_____ the likely culprits.
5. _____**Their**_____ tickets to Singapore are first class.
6. I can't find _____**their**_____ address.
7. _____**There**_____ is a detour due to construction just up the road.
8. _____**There**_____ wasn't anything worth watching on television.
9. _____**They're**_____ not to be trusted.
10. _____**Their**_____ first choice of vacation spots was Maui.
11. _____**There**_____ will be a fifteen minute break at four o'clock.
12. Did you see _____**their**_____ reaction?

Write one sentence for each of the words *their, there,* and *they're.*

13. (their) _I like their work._

14. (there) _There are my shoes._

15. (they're) _They're wonderful people._

© Carson-Dellosa CD-3744   83

Name _____ Word Usage

Your and You're

Your is the possessive form of "you." **You're** is the contraction for "you are."

> Example: I know your secret. (the secret belongs to you)
> <u>You're</u> the people's choice. (contraction of "you are")

Correctly fill in the blank with *your* or *you're.*

1. I don't know _____**your**_____ name.
2. _____**You're**_____ the cause of all this.
3. I am impressed with _____**your**_____ proposal.
4. I don't like what _____**you're**_____ thinking.
5. _____**Your**_____ suggestion is a good one.
6. _____**You're**_____ not serious!
7. _____**You're**_____ the most likely applicant to get the position.
8. I think that these are _____**your**_____ earrings.
9. Is that _____**your**_____ dog?
10. _____**You're**_____ the only one left.
11. What is _____**your**_____ social security number?
12. Is _____**your**_____ decision made?
13. _____**You're**_____ perfect for the part.
14. What is _____**your**_____ opinion?
15. _____**You're**_____ welcome to come.
16. I found _____**your**_____ sweater in my closet.

© Carson-Dellosa CD-3744   84

Answer Pages

Name _____ Word Usage

Its and _It's_

It's is a contraction for _It is_ or _it has_. **Its** is the possessive form of _it_.

Example: It's the wrong phone number. (contraction of _it is_)
The neighborhood lost its electrical power. (power belongs to _it_)

Correctly fill in each blank with _it's_ or _its_.

1. __It's__ time to make a decision.
2. The navy squadron must follow __its__ orders.
3. Do you know __its__ brand name?
4. __It's__ the wrong path.
5. Virtue is __its__ own reward.
6. Do you know if __it's__ time to go?
7. __Its__ odor is unmistakable.
8. __Its__ value has not yet been determined.
9. No one is sure of __its__ origin.
10. __It's__ still broken.
11. Everything was in __its__ place.
12. __Its__ cause was unclear.
13. __It's__ my sister's bicycle.
14. __It's__ not your concern.
15. If __it's__ raining, we'll call off the hike.

Name _____ Word Usage

Than and _Then_

Then is an adverb of time. **Than** is a conjunction used in clauses of comparison.

Example: She then finished her homework. (tells when she finished)
She felt better today than yesterday . (compares _today_ and _yesterday_)

Fill in each blank using _then_ or _than_ correctly.

1. The watch costs more now __than__ it did two weeks ago.
2. He thought that he could handle the money better __than__ I could.
3. And __then__ there were none.
4. You go first, __then__ I'll go.
5. You pick it out, __then__ I'll buy it.
6. I'd rather go tonight __than__ this afternoon.
7. The cat would rather be snoozing __than__ playing.
8. Bob enjoys basketball more __than__ fishing.
9. Marinate the steak, and __then__ put it in the refrigerator overnight.
10. Hubert plays piano better __than__ Jeremy.
11. Turn on the computer, __then__ open the file.
12. If you go, __then__ I'll go too.
13. __Then__ it will be Mark's turn.
14. Do you know what happened __then__?
15. I like the fir tree more __than__ the spruce tree.

Name _____ Word Usage

Double Negatives

One negative word makes an entire sentence negative. Using a second negative word (**double negative**) in the same sentence is not acceptable. _Barely, scarcely, never,_ and _hardly_ are considered negatives, as well as _not, no, no one_ and _nothing_.

Example: I scarcely got no sleep last night. (double negative is incorrect)
I scarcely got any sleep last night. (correct)

Rewrite each sentence so that there is not a double negative.

1. I couldn't hardly wait for summer camp.
   I could hardly wait for summer camp.

2. Valerie never had no acceptable excuses for her frequent tardiness.
   Valerie never had acceptable excuses for her frequent tardiness.

3. Clarice didn't never see him again.
   Clarice never did see him again.

4. My parents said that there wasn't no way that I could go.
   My parents said that there was no way that I could go.

5. Nothing never thrilled me more than my first sight of Notre Dame Cathedral in Paris.
   Nothing ever thrilled me more than my first sight of Notre Dame Cathedral in Paris.

6. No one had nothing to say about the incident.
   No one had anything to say about the incident.

7. I hadn't never realized how destructive gossip could be.
   I had never realized how destructive gossip could be.

8. I don't like to play no card games.
   I don't like to play any card games.

Name _____ Capitalization

Capitalization of Titles

Capitalize the title of books, movies, poems, songs, television programs, and works of art. Do not capitalize words such as _the, and, on, by,_ and _of_ unless they are the first word in the title.

Rewrite the titles in the sentences that follow using capitals correctly.

1. (_mutiny on the bounty_) __Mutiny on the Bounty__, written by Nordhoff and Hal, is possibly the greatest sea story of all time.

2. (_the hobbit_) __The Hobbit__ is a fantasy written by J.R. Tolkien which is enjoyed by children and adults alike.

3. (_sunset boulevard_) __Sunset Boulevard__, the musical sensation, was written by Andrew Lloyd Webber.

4. (_lord of the flies_) In 1954 William Golding wrote a book entitled __Lord of the Flies__ about a group of English school boys stranded without adults on a desert island.

5. (_paradise lost_) John Milton wrote an epic poem called __Paradise Lost__ about the creation of the world.

6. (_the cosby show_) One of the most popular family sitcoms of all times was __The Cosby Show__.

7. (_stopping by the woods on a snowy evening_) One of the most musical and haunting poems written by Robert Frost is __Stopping by the Woods on a Snowy Evening__.

8. (_roll of thunder, hear my cry_) Mildred Taylor, who won the 1977 Newbery Medal for her realistic portrayal of black family life in rural Mississippi in the early 1930s, dedicated the book __Roll of Thunder, Hear My Cry__ to the memory of her father.

Answer Pages

Name _____   **Capitalization**

Word Capitalization

Use an initial capital letter to mark proper nouns (Ben Franklin), or adjectives (Chinese), titles of distinction (Prince of Wales), races, religions, and ethnic groups (Caucasian, Buddhist), official bodies (the United States Senate), and geographic divisions (the East Side).

Underline the word(s) that should be capitalized.

1. <u>hans holzer</u>, a famous psychic investigator, has written a number of books on ghosts and writes on this topic regularly for national magazines, motion pictures, and television.
2. He has investigated haunted places in <u>europe</u> from <u>scotland</u> to <u>austria</u> and has many tales to tell.
3. One of the most celebrated haunted places is the <u>tower</u> of <u>london.</u>
4. <u>anne boleyn</u>, the second wife of <u>henry viii</u> who was beheaded for supposed infidelity, has been seen walking headless in the <u>salt tower</u> in the <u>tower</u> of <u>london.</u>
5. <u>longleat</u> in <u>somerset</u> is one of the most publicized haunted houses in <u>england</u>.
6. It seems that at least four ghosts haunt this stately dwelling: the <u>lady louisa</u>, who mourned the violent death of her lover, the slaughtered rebel from the <u>duke</u> of <u>mon mouth's</u> army, the builder of longleat, <u>sir john thynne</u>, and the wealthy owner, <u>thomas thynne</u>, who was murdered by a certain <u>lieutenant stern.</u>
7. In <u>scotland</u> is a small house by the name of <u>croft-en-reigh</u> which stands in back of <u>holyrood palace</u>, once the residence of <u>mary queen</u> of <u>scots.</u>
8. Her ghost, who had often been to this house in times of great emotional turmoil, has supposedly been seen here, as well as the sixteenth century <u>french</u> architect who built the place.
9. Another <u>european</u> haunted house is <u>ross house</u> in <u>ireland</u>, which stands on a bluff looking directly into <u>clew bay</u>, halfway between <u>westport</u> and <u>newport.</u>
10. One ghost is that of a maid in a starched blue and white uniform named <u>annie o'flynn</u>, who was a very loyal servant to one of the former families.
11. Another former owner who has been frequently observed in the garden and on the stairs at <u>ross house</u> is the sea captain, who died at sea, but has been observed by many, always in the daylight, and always smoking a cigar.
12. One haunted site in <u>france</u>, built during the <u>second empire</u> in the 1860s by <u>emperor napoleon iii</u>, is located in the suburbs of <u>paris.</u>
13. <u>napoleon</u> kept a lonely mistress there, and she played her grand piano constantly.
14. Until the house was finally abandoned, numerous people who slept there in the <u>parisian</u> suburb of <u>maison-lafitte</u> heard loud nocturnal music from their bedrooms above the salon that contained the grand piano.

Name _____   **Commas**

Commas to Separate Dates and Addresses

Use commas to separate parts of dates and addresses. Do not separate the ZIP code from the city and state with a comma.

Example: The battle of New Orleans was fought on March 13, 1815.
The New York Convention and Visitor's Bureau is located at:
2 Columbus Circle, New York, New York 10019.
We left on Monday, July 5th.

Add commas to correctly complete the following sentences.

1. The package was sent on November 11,1994, but did not arrive until January 4,1996.
2. Mr. Harper's retirement will begin on Monday, April 11,1997.
3. The Duponts will stay at a hotel at 40 Avenue Victor Hugo, Aix-en-Provence,France.
4. If you think nothing of spending $500.00 for a pair of shoes, go to Via Veneto 98, Rome,Italy to shop.
5. Her pen pal's address is 4700 Main Street,Kansas City,Kansas 22980.
6. The first performance of Giuseppe Verdi's Rigoletto was at La Fenice Theatre in Venice on March 11,1851.
7. The address on the postcard was 81 Mariani Avenue,Cupertino,California 95014-6299.
8. Which catalog company is located at 1 Lands' End,Dodgeville,Wisconsin 53539?
9. The baby was born on April 19,1995 in Mobile Alabama.
10. My new job begins in September in Grand Rapids,Michigan.
11. The September 14,1991 issue of *Time* has an article on the presidential candidates.
12. On Saturday July 17,1995 my sister married her high school sweetheart.
13. The deposit for the senior class trip is due no later than Friday, February 3 ,1995.
14. Please send all entries to 501 Post Street,San Francisco,California 94102.
15. I will always remember Christmas,1972.
16. Send your resume to P.O. Box 89710,Dallas,Texas 75202.
17. My dentist appointment is set for 3 o'clock on Monday,March 15.
18. Many Gulf Coast resorts are located on Sandestin Boulevard South in Destin,Florida.

Name _____   **Punctuation**

Commas to Separate Independent Clauses

Use a comma to separate independent clauses joined by the coordinating conjunctions: *and, but, yet, nor,* or *yet* unless each clause is very short.

Example: Brad will bring a variety of snacks, and Sarah will bring three or four videos.
The sky darkened and the rain fell. (two short independent clauses)
The sky darkened and sounded menacing. (only one independent clause)

Place commas where appropriate in each sentence. Leave the sentence blank if no punctuation is needed.

1. The time was midnight, and my homework still wasn't finished.
2. She agrees and he disagrees.
3. I did not know her name, but she looked very familiar.
4. Whales are mammals, and they must come to the surface of the water for air.
5. We waited in front of the school, but our ride did not come.
6. Frank heard the news, and he quickly told his friends.
7. Celeste looked everywhere, but her bracelet was gone.
8. We could go Christmas shopping today, or we could wait until the weekend.
9. Are you planning to attend college in town, or will you be looking elsewhere?
10. The hotel room had a beautiful view, but it was too small.
11. We were exhausted, yet we couldn't get to sleep.
12. That test should be very difficult, or I shall be surprised.
13. Parking downtown is a nuisance, and it is very expensive.
14. Sean is a good writer, but he is a lousy typist.
15. The choice seems obvious, yet I can't decide.
16. The Jacksons love skiing, and they go every winter.
17. I went skiing once, but I wasn't very good at it.
18. Will you be coming with my sister or driving yourself?
19. Carl likes fishing, but Victor prefers mountain climbing.
20. Our home is rather small, but we don't mind.

Name _____   **Punctuation**

Commas to Separate Dependent from Independent Clauses

Use a comma to separate a dependent (subordinate) clause from the main clause when the subordinate clause comes first.

Example: Before Kern began her recipe, she made sure she had all the ingredients.

Place commas where appropriate.

1. Although I like snow skiing, exploring the ruins of a Gothic castle is my favorite.
2. While Crystal swam many laps, Bob sunbathed.
3. Because they cater to teens, these shops are not too expensive.
4. When I finally passed the big sign welcoming me to Window Rock,Arizona,I noticed that I was out of gas.
5. Since she loves rugged sports, Norma would like to try paragliding.
6. If you enjoy German cooking, try sauerbraten.
7. While we relaxed on our hotel balcony, we enjoyed a panoramic vista of Santa Fe and spectacular views of the Sangre de Cristo Mountains.
8. After we visited a museum, we had lunch at a sunny outdoor cafe.
9. Because they see divers so constantly, the green sea turtles which live in the Sheraton Caverns in Kauai, Hawaii are not afraid of people.
10. While most wild animals prefer flight to fight, you must consider that they can be dangerous and unpredictable.
11. As the terrain opened up below me, I nearly fell off my chair in the ski lift.
12. Since I love to write, my Brazilian pen pal and I exchanged countless letters.
13. If you enjoy snowmobile races, try the Iron Dog Race between Wasilla and Nome, Alaska.
14. Until Snowshoe Thompson took the job of mailman-on-skis in 1856 in the Sierra Nevada, there had been virtually no communication between the remote mining towns and the rest of the world in the winter.
15. If you hate cold feet, it is possible to buy a compact, battery-operated foot warming system.

Answer Pages

© Carson-Dellosa CD-3744

Page 93

Name _____   Punctuation

Commas with Introductory Prepositional Phrase

Use a comma following two or more introductory prepositional phrases.

Example: In the afternoon after lunch, we visited the museum.

Insert a comma where needed. Leave the sentence blank if it is already correct.

1. In spite of the warning about the bad weather, Albert went boating anyway.

2. Tomorrow afternoon we will pick up Jack and his family at the airport.

3. With the money in her hand, she bought the expensive car with the convertible top.

4. After the beginning of the parade, we decided that it was too crowded and left.

5. In the darkness in front of the car, I saw a wild animal quickly dart across the road.

6. At dinner Patty told us the good news and made us promise to keep it a secret.

7. Around the corner there is a gourmet grocery store.

8. On the freshly mopped floor a long trail of fresh dog prints could be seen.

9. With the increase in price, we decided to settle for a less expensive model.

10. After the long, hot summer we were happy to welcome the brisk fall weather.

11. In spite of my vehement protests, the policeman gave me a speeding ticket.

12. The girl the in the picture wearing the lavender velvet dress is my youngest sister.

13. Across the table sat a man with a sour expression on his bearded face.

14. Between Birch and Pine Street is a neighborhood grocery store, dry cleaners, and drug store.

15. After June of this year, Ms. Jackson will be able to retire from teaching.

© Carson-Dellosa CD-3744   93

Page 94

Name _____   Punctuation

Commas with Interrupters

Commas are used to set apart expressions that interrupt a sentence. These include: appositives and appositive phrases, words used in direct address, and parenthetical expressions or other interrupters that are not essential to the meaning of the sentence (such as *however, on the other hand, obviously, in my opinion, of course,* or *therefore*).

Example: We saw Bill, the new kid, standing by his locker. (appositive phrase)
Paul, I hold you responsible for this. (direct address)
This pie, in my opinion, should win the blue ribbon. (parenthetical expressions)

Place commas where needed. In the blank, tell if the comma separates an appositive or appositive phrase (A), a direct address (D), or parenthetical expressions (P).

_P_ 1. The answer, of course, is twenty-one.

_A_ 2. Sarah, the tallest girl, is a great volleyball player.

_D_ 3. I told you, Brandon, to leave me alone.

_A_ 4. *Sunset Boulevard,* Andrew Lloyd Webber's latest musical, is playing to packed houses in New York and London.

_D_ 5. The murderer, my dear Watson, must be a woman.

_A_ 6. Le Petit Theatre du Vieux Carre, the oldest theatre in the south, is located in New Orleans.

_D_ 7. Fido, stop that barking!

_P_ 8. Jessica Lange, in my opinion, should have won the Oscar.

_D_ 9. Barry, call your sister to the phone.

_D_ 10. I told you, Ann, to stop putting it off.

_A_ 11. George Bailey, a man with high ideals, is a beloved character from a movie called *It's a Wonderful Life.*

_A_ 12. Mrs. Clark, the hardest seventh grade English teacher, gave me an A on my essay.

© Carson-Dellosa CD-3744   94

Page 95

Name _____   Punctuation

Quotation Marks

Quotation marks enclose the words used by a speaker or writer. Periods and commas go inside the closing quotation mark in the preferred American style. A comma is used to set off a direct from the rest of the sentence. Question marks and exclamation points go inside the closing quotation marks only when they apply to the quoted words. Indirect quotations do not use quotation marks.

Example: "Come here," said Marie. (comma inside)
Marie said, "Come here." (comma used to set off direct quote, period inside)
"Won't you come?" asked Marie. (question mark inside)
Did you hear Marie ask, "Won't you come"? (question mark outside)
Marie asked that I come. (indirect quotation)

Rewrite each sentence using quotation marks, punctuation, and capitalization where needed. Do not change indirect quotations.

1. What happened to you asked Melissa.
   "What happened to you?" asked Melissa.

2. I slipped and sprained my ankle responded Nina.
   "I slipped and sprained my ankle," responded Nina.

3. Melissa asked how she had sprained her ankle.
   Melissa asked how she had sprained her ankle.

4. Nina confessed it was my new spiked-heel shoes.
   "It was my new spiked-heel shoes," Nina Confessed.

5. I warned you about those things chided Melissa.
   "I warned you about those things," chided Melissa.

6. But they look so good on me insisted Nina.
   "But they look so good on me!" insisted Nina.

© Carson-Dellosa CD-3744   95

Page 96

Name _____   Punctuation

Indirect and Direct Quotations

Quotation marks enclose the words used by a speaker or writer. Periods and commas go inside the closing quotation mark in the preferred American style. A comma is used to set off a direct from the rest of the sentence. Question marks and exclamation points go inside the closing quotation marks only when they apply to the quoted words. Indirect quotations do not use quotation marks.

Example: "I like this book," said Paula. (comma inside)
Paula said, "Come here." (comma used to set off direct quote, period inside)
"What is your anme?" asked Stevan. (question mark inside)
Did you hear Carol ask, "What is your name"? (question mark outside)
Debbie asked me to bring this.. (indirect quotation)

Rewrite the indirect quotations as direct quotations. Rewrite the direct quotations as indirect quotations.

1. The waiter said that the entree would be out shortly.
   The waiter said," The entreé will be out shortly."

2. "Do you know her pediatrician?" asked Mr. Howell.
   Mr. Howell asked if he knew her pediatrcian.

3. She suddenly asked where I was going.
   She suddenly asked, "Where are you going?"

4. "Can I help you?" asked the saleslady.
   The saleslady asked if she could help her.

5. Maxwell said, " I also need four trays of pansies and some mulch."
   Maxwell said that he also needed four trays of pansies and some mulch.

6. The teacher requested that everyone bring two number 2 pencils for the exam.
   "Bring two number 2 pencils for the exam," the teacher requested.

© Carson-Dellosa CD-3744   96

Answer Pages

Comma Review

Add commas as needed to the following passage.

Many people dream of seeing lions, elephants, and cheetahs in the wild, but an African Safari takes you into the best game preserves for life-size encounters with these amazing creatures. Kenya and Tanzania, two areas in Africa famous for their safari adventures, provide good starting points.

Before you embark on your first safari, you should prepare yourself by attending a presentation on national park reserves and wildlife given by the East African Wild Life Society. Founded in 1961, the East African Wildlife Society uses the proceeds from membership fees to support research and education, to conduct surveys and anti-poaching patrols, and to rescue and relocate endangered animals. The presentation will help you to more fully understand and appreciate what lies ahead.

The most common way to travel in a safari is by minibus, and there is a roof hatch for stand-up viewing for those who care to get an unobstructed view of the animals. Don't worry. Everyone has a window seat, and there are ample photo opportunities.

The Samburu Game Reserve, named for the tribe living in the area, is a popular area for safaris. One animal that you will undoubtedly see is the seemingly tame olive baboon. Other seldom seen wildlife in this preserve include the thin-striped Gervy's zebra, reticulated giraffe, blue-necked Somali ostrich, and Beisa oryx.

Another spectacular place for viewing is Aberdare National Park. It contains the world-famous lodges, Treetops and The Ark, known for their salt licks and water holes where wildlife come to drink. You can watch the animals that come from the comfort of your viewing deck for as long as you like.

For a once-in-a-lifetime opportunity, make reservations for an early morning hot air balloon ride over the Serengeti Plain. Masai Mara, the northern extension of Tanzania's Serengeti, is home to vast herds of plains game such as wildebeest, zebra, antelope, and gazelle. This afternoon of game viewing takes you to the animals' favorite haunts, including the wooded area, riverbanks and vast grassy plains.

If you haven't had your fill, go to Olduvai Gorge where Dr. Leakey discovered a skull reputed to be from an early hominid. Here you will see the Ngorongoro Crater, an extinct collapsed volcano. The crater's floor is 102 square miles, and there is a lake in the center. An all terrain vehicle drive you through the crater floor where lions, elephants, rhinos, leopards, water buffaloes, hyenas, and cheetahs abound.

    97

Capitals, Commas, and Quotation Marks Review

Read the following conversation. Underline any word that needs a capital letter. Add commas and quotation marks as needed in each sentence.

1. "How would you like to go with me on a four day cruise of the galapagos Islands?" Max casually remarked to matthew.
2. "Sure, why not?" responded Matthew.
3. "By the way, max, what will we be seeing there?"
4. "How about marine iguana, sea lions, giant tortoises, frigate birds, and strange rock formations?" suggested Max.
5. Max asked Matthew, rather sheepishly, "Where are the galapagos Islands?"
6. "Well, first we will need to get to Quito, Ecuador's capital, which rests at an altitude of 9,350 feet in the andes Mountains."
7. "The Galapagos Islands are right off shore from Quito, I suppose," suggested matthew.
8. "No, not really," said Max, "we still have quite a way to go."
9. Max continued, "Next we'll take the Expreso Metropolitan train through the Andes Mountains down devil's Nose, a nearly vertical 1,000 foot cliff."
10. "Cool," replied Matthew.
11. "From there," continued Max, "we will come to the flatlands of the coastal jungle where we'll catch a small plane, and we'll fly over the Pacific to baltra Isle."
12. "That is where we will board the cruise boat, I suppose," said Matthew.
13. "Right, Baltra is in the center of the fifteen island Galapagos archipelago, and we'll cruise for four days through these volcanic islands."
14. "After going to all that trouble to get there, I hope we'll be seeing something really unusual," Matthew stated.
15. "How about some land iguanas, a forest of opuntia cactus, and some blue-footed boobies?"
16. "Okay, I've got to admit that you've captured my interest," said Matthew, "What else will we see?"
17. "On the beach of Punta suarex, I hear that there is something called the waved albatross with a wingspan of eight feet," offered Max, "and there are giant tortoises in the interior of the santa cruz island."
18. "Personally I'm most interested in Puerta Egas where we'll be surrounded by marine iguana, pelicans, sea lions, penguins, and fur seals," continued Max with his endless information.

    98

---

noun 1	pronoun 2	verb 3	adjective 4
© CD-3744	© CD-3744	© CD-3744	© CD-3744
adverb 5	preposition 6	conjunction 7	interjection 8
© CD-3744	© CD-3744	© CD-3744	© CD-3744
simple past 9	simple present 10	simple future 11	past perfect 12
© CD-3744	© CD-3744	© CD-3744	© CD-3744
present perfect 13	future perfect 14	Brian had given that lecture to a group once before. 15	That blue flower is much larger than the yellow one. 16
© CD-3744	© CD-3744	© CD-3744	© CD-3744

Kelly has believed that
story since third grade.

20

That letter has been
mailed to you.

24

The dog has been
howling all night.

28

They will have been
working for hours by the
time we deliver the food.

32

I will have taken the test
by next Monday.

19

We will have begun the
project before March.

23

I will remember your kind
deeds.

27

The doorbell will alert
me when you arrive.

31

She had run the race in
under three minutes.

18

The family built
a strong business.

22

The city will have
expanded in a few more
years.

26

The scientist reported his
findings.

30

Kedric behaves well in
science class.

17

The party was held
in the gym.

21

We had to leave for the
baseball game.

25

He had heard that rumor
last week.

29

The meeting has ended.

33

I had emptied the wastebasket already.

34

Roy had eaten the whole chicken before I sat down.

35

I did my homework last night.

36

The man will paint the garage today.

37

Faye had worn those shoes to the last party.

38

I have done all of the cleaning.

39

simple subject

40

simple predicate

41

complete subject

42

complete predicate

43

compound simple subject

44

compound simple predicate

45

compound complete subject

46

compound complete predicate

47

simple subject and complete predicate

48

complete subject and simple predicate 49 © CD-3744	**compound subject and simple predicate** 50 © CD-3744	**complete subject and complete predicate** 51 © CD-3744	**simple subject and compound complete predicate** 52 © CD-3744
Compound simple subject and compound simple predicate 53 © CD-3744	**compound complete subject and compound complete predicate** 54 © CD-3744	**S-V** 55 © CD-3744	**S-V-O** 56 © CD-3744
S-V-IO-DO 57 © CD-3744	**S-LV-PN** 58 © CD-3744	**S-LV-PA** 59 © CD-3744	subject | predicate 60 © CD-3744

subject / subject — and — verb 61 © CD-3744

subject — verb and verb 62 © CD-3744

subject \| verb \| direct object 63 © CD-3744

subject \| verb \| direct object / indirect object 64 © CD-3744

65.

subject | linking verb / predicate adjective

© CD-3744

66.

subject | linking verb / predicate nominative

© CD-3744

67.

verb / adverb

© CD-3744

68.

verb / adverb / adverb

© CD-3744

69.

noun / adjective / adverb

© CD-3744

70.

noun / prep / object of preposition

© CD-3744

71.

verb / prep / object of preposition

© CD-3744

72. The cat eats after our meal.

© CD-3744

73. The cold weather brought heavy snow.

© CD-3744

74. Joe's sister is the center of attention.

© CD-3744

75. The woman gave Paula a warning look.

© CD-3744

76. Her face turned red.

© CD-3744

77. The cake tasted rather sweet.

© CD-3744

78. Fred and Ronald attend a school in Iowa.

© CD-3744

79. Bart will race for our team and probably win.

© CD-3744

80. We ate a wonderful meal at your house yesterday.

© CD-3744

independent clause

dependent clause

81 — I saw a gray turtle in my backyard last week.
© CD-3744

82
© CD-3744

83
© CD-3744

84 — she brought the package with a red ribbon
© CD-3744

85 — he would rather eat at a restaurant
© CD-3744

86 — below the window and over the shelf
© CD-3744

87 — he reads the paper daily
© CD-3744

88 — who slipped on the icy sidewalk
© CD-3744

89 — near the book and next to the pencil
© CD-3744

90 — the television program was entertaining
© CD-3744

91 — the antics of the crowd made a gleeful scene
© CD-3744

92 — before we hid inside the closet
© CD-3744

93 — the club meets afer school on Tuesdays
© CD-3744

94 — we walked the path through the woods
© CD-3744

95 — while I tied the laces on my shoes
© CD-3744

96 — the answer was found in the chapter
© CD-3744